"In this book, Lynn really speaks to teachers, recognising the lack of initial training to support the positive teaching of autistic children, but also the crucial part teachers and para-professionals can play in supporting autistic children to thrive.
The focus on 'getting it right from the start' in Year 7 acknowledges the transitional difficulties many autistic young people experience but offers practical guidance on how to make this successful. What practitioners will particularly value is the contextual positioning alongside government policy which ensures practice is reflective of national priorities. This is, quite simply, a 'must read' for all secondary subject teachers."

– **Nicola Crossley**, CEO NAS Academies Trust and National SEND Representative for ASCL

"This is a book that any Secondary teacher or SENCO will find invaluable as a tool to support good inclusive practice. It relates to subject teachers and shows understanding of the pressures but gives easy to understand and implement solutions."

– **Sally Glossop**, Lead for the Graduated Response, Herts County Council

"I wish this book had been written in my own childhood, it would have saved me many years of misery, dread and at times fear of going to school. It would have stopped the teachers from writing on my reports, 'Hilary is a below average pupil and must try harder' and 'Hilary is very quiet and needs to contribute more to class discussions.' This needs to be mandatory reading for everyone involved in secondary education, so that all autistic young people can have the support they need, so that they can enjoy learning, and to feel positive about their future."

– **Hilary Forbes**, Mathematics Tutor and Specialist Autism Consultant, Reachout ASC

"If you are a secondary practitioner looking to better understand and support the needs of autistic learners, then look no further. Driven by the voices and experiences of autistic students, this book is brimming with practical advice for best practice. It also offers invaluable insights into what's needed to create accessible learning environments where autistic learners are not only understood and supported but also valued and celebrated."

–**Dean Beadle**, autistic speaker, trainer and writer

"Lynn's dedication to making the world a better place for autistic people shines through this book from every page. This, combined with her understanding of what it is like to be a teacher in a busy classroom with a million things on your to-do list already, makes this book a super practical guide. If you want to do better by the autistic children in your classroom then this is the book for you."

– **Joanna Grace**, Sensory Engagement and Inclusion specialist and Founder of The Sensory Projects

"Lynn's research and work with autistic people has once again informed her excellent books. The work with autistic young people, doing 'what's right for me' is outstanding in achieving best practice for those young people and beyond to their families and classmates. I would recommend both the primary and secondary editions to inform and enable all school staff to fully understand and support the young people in their care."

– **Dawn Brown**, SEND Assistant Head, Hertfordshire

"This is an excellent and timely book, that will be well received by new teachers, support staff, and more experienced professionals. Written in an easy-to-read format, and addressing many of the key areas of challenge autistic learners encounter in secondary schools every day, the book draws on the vast experiences of the author alongside those of autistic young people.
The book is packed full of first-hand advice and lived experience, covering a vast range of topics with practical advice and solutions. I am certain that if you are a new professional or experienced colleague, this book will help improve the outcomes of the autistic young people you teach."

- **Gareth Morewood**, Educational Advisor and former secondary SENCO

"Lynn McCann *gets it*. I have always been struck by her insight into autistic experiences of school, and her ability to translate them into classroom strategies that teachers can easily pick up. Her commitment to listening to autistic people, and learning from us, shine through in her work and in the many quotes used for illumination. This book makes a clear, compelling and concise case for how to make schools truly inclusive for autistic learners."

- **Fergus Murray**, Science Teacher and Chair, Autistic Mutual Aid Society Edinburgh (AMASE)

"A much needed book that shares with secondary school teachers WHY autistic teens find a lot of school more difficult than their non-autistic peers in their own words. It is wise, kind, and deeply practical in its approach. It has quick wins for teaching autistic children and what things to avoid. The book includes vital areas that must be dealt with differently for autistic pupils such as sex and relationship education. Lynn shares a range of helpful strategies from supporting children settle in Year 7, and classroom management, to how to help them to do their best in exams."

- **Sarah-Jane Critchley**, author, speaker, consultant, coach

All About Autism (Secondary) is accompanied by a number of printable online materials, designed to ensure this resource best supports your professional needs.

Go to https://resourcecentre.routledge.com/speechmark and click on the cover of this book.

Answer the question prompt using your copy of the book to gain access to the online content.

ALL ABOUT AUTISM

All About Autism is an accessible and informative guide for secondary school teachers, designed to increase their knowledge and understanding of autism and enhance their toolkit with practical, adaptable strategies to support autistic learners in their care.

The book initially explores key traits and terminology, debunks myths and misconceptions, and shines a light on the strengths and abilities of autistic learners. It then introduces readers to a range of easy-to-implement ideas for practice and concrete solutions to provide further support, all with the child at the heart. *All About Autism* includes:

- Practical strategies tailored to the secondary key stages with current research broken down into easily digestible chunks.
- A focus on adaptive teaching and how to implement key strategies in different subject areas.
- Guidance on a range of topics, from supporting students with mental health and anxiety to managing group work, class work, writing difficulties, homework and exams.
- Strategies to support an understanding of puberty, relationships and sex education.
- Approaches to foster autistic pride and to promote positive attitudes to diversity in all its forms.
- Easy to dip in and out of chapters with signposting to further research, resources and support.

Taking a celebratory approach, the guide focuses on difference rather than deficit and weaves together the voices of autistic learners and parents alongside practical examples of what high-quality and adapted teaching should look like. It will be essential reading for all secondary school educators, SENCOs and parents who are supporting autistic learners aged 11–16.

Lynn McCann has been a teacher for 32 years and in that time has worked as a mainstream teacher, SENCO and for eight years was a class and outreach teacher in an autism specialist school. She set up Reachout ASC in 2014 after realising that there was a great need for good, practical, specialist support in mainstream schools. It is an independent service that specialises in autism, ADHD and PDA support, with children's voices at the heart of all they do.

ALL ABOUT SEND

Series Advisor: Natalie Packer

All About SEND provides busy teachers and SENCOs with essential guidance and practical strategies to effectively support learners with special educational needs and disabilities. Each accessible and informative book focuses on a common area of need and explores key traits and terminology, debunks myths and misconceptions and introduces readers to a range of easy-to-implement ideas for practice and concrete solutions to everyday challenges.

ALL ABOUT AUTISM
A Practical Guide for Primary Teachers
Lynn McCann

ALL ABOUT AUTISM
A Practical Guide for Secondary Teachers
Lynn McCann

ALL ABOUT AUTISM

A PRACTICAL GUIDE FOR SECONDARY TEACHERS

Lynn McCann

LONDON AND NEW YORK

Designed cover image: © Getty Images

First published 2023
by Routledge
4 Park Square, Milton Park, Abingdon, Oxon OX14 4RN

and by Routledge
605 Third Avenue, New York, NY 10158

Routledge is an imprint of the Taylor & Francis Group, an informa business

British Library Cataloguing-in-Publication Data
A catalogue record for this book is available from the British Library

ISBN: 978-1-032-24780-9 (hbk)
ISBN: 978-1-032-24781-6 (pbk)
ISBN: 978-1-003-28007-1 (ebk)

DOI: 10.4324/9781003280071

Typeset in Interstate
by Deanta Global Publishing Services, Chennai, India

Access the online resources: https://resourcecentre.routledge.com/speechmark

CONTENTS

FOREWORD

All teachers are teachers of learners with Special Educational Needs and Disabilities (SEND). Those professionals who work in truly inclusive schools will understand that SEND is everyone's responsibility. However, the situation has not always been like this. When I started my teaching career 32 years ago, learners who had additional needs were more likely to be seen as the responsibility of the Special Educational Needs Co-ordinator (SENCO). As the person in school who 'held' the SEND knowledge and expertise, the SENCO would often be a lone force in championing, and meeting, the needs of this particular group of learners.

The picture in education is somewhat different today. The profile of the children and young people we teach continues to change. The impact of the Covid pandemic, for example, has led to an increase in those identified with gaps in their learning, or with mental health concerns. The number of learners with complex needs being educated within mainstream schools also continues to rise. As professionals, we now have a greater awareness and understanding of some of the challenges our learners face and, as a result, are more determined to do our best to support them to achieve. We understand that this cannot be the role of one person - the SENCO - alone. Every teacher needs to be a teacher of SEND.

Teaching learners with SEND may be one of the most rewarding things you ever do in your classroom. When you observe a learner who has really struggled to grasp a new idea or concept finally achieve their 'lightbulb moment,' it's all the more sweet knowing the amount of effort they have put in to get there. However, teaching learners with SEND can also be one of the most challenging aspects of your career. In a 2019 survey[1] carried out by the Department for Education (DfE) in England, the level of confidence amongst teachers in supporting learners with SEND was reported as very low. Relevant professional development in this area is, at best, patchy; only 41% of the teachers surveyed by the DfE felt there was sufficient SEND training in place for all teachers.

So how do we overcome this challenge? Evidence suggests that the best place to start is through the delivery of inclusive, High Quality Teaching (HQT). As the Education Endowment Foundation (EEF) report[2] tells us, there is no 'magic bullet' for teaching learners with SEND and to a great extent, good teaching for those with SEND is good teaching for all. This means we need to develop a repertoire of effective teaching strategies such as scaffolding, explicit instruction and use of technology, then use these strategies flexibly to meet the needs of individuals or groups of learners.

Although a focus on effective, HQT in the classroom is the starting point, some learners will require more specific teaching methods to meet their individual needs. There is no substitute for really getting to know a child or young person so you can fully understand their personal strengths, potential barriers to learning and what works for them in the classroom. However, it can still be helpful for us as professionals to develop a more general understanding of some of the common areas of need we are likely to come across and to have a range of strategies we can try implementing within our practice. This is where *All About SEND* can help.

The *All About SEND* series of books aims to support every teacher to be a teacher of SEND. Each book has been designed to enable teachers, and other professionals such as support staff, to develop their knowledge and understanding of how to effectively promote teaching and learning for those with identified areas of need. The books provide essential information and a range of practical strategies for supporting learners in the classroom. Written by expert practitioners, the guidance has been informed by a wealth of first-hand experience, with the views of children and young people with SEND and their parents taking centre stage.

In this book, *All About Autism*, the author Lynn McCann provides essential guidance on supporting autistic learners in the secondary classroom. As Director of Reachout ASC autism outreach service, Lynn has vast experience of working directly with autistic learners and their families and in supporting schools to develop excellent autism-friendly practice. Written from a very child-centred viewpoint, *All About Autism* provides a range of extremely practical, tried-and-tested ideas based on what really works for autistic learners in the classroom.

Thank you for choosing to read this book and for embracing the challenge of responsibility: every teacher a teacher of SEND.

Natalie Packer
All About SEND Series Advisor
SEND Consultant, Director of NPEC Ltd.
@NataliePacker

NOTES

1. https://assets.publishing.service.gov.uk/government/uploads/system/uploads/attachment_data/file/1063620/SEND_review_right_support_right_place_right_time_accessible.pdf pg. 42.
2. https://educationendowmentfoundation.org.uk/education-evidence/guidance-reports/send.

ACKNOWLEDGEMENTS

Writing any book like this cannot happen without the help of the teachers, parents and most of all the autistic children I have worked with over the past ten years or more. Working with so many dedicated people who are committed to making school successful for all children has been a joy. We all know the realities of an education system still trying to recover from a pandemic as I write this in 2022, and a SEND system that seems increasingly unable to provide the resources to make education accessible and successful for all children. But we teachers have a lot of creativity and hope. We do this job because we want to see children thrive and I hope this book will help you understand and make that difference for your autistic pupils this and every year. Thank you for reading this book and wanting to learn from the children and teachers I have worked with in their schools.

I want to thank the following schools who have given me permission to use scenarios from their practice in this book:

Ripley St Thomas Academy, Lancaster
Hutton Grammar School, Preston

And the following organisations or individuals who have given me permission to use quotes from their surveys and children who are autistic:

Spectrum Gaming (Andy Smith and his team) www.spectrumgaming.net
And the pupils I have worked with over the past ten years who told me what school is like for them but wanted to remain anonymous.

Autistic adults I have supported or worked with:

Cristina Mylroie
Jackson Watkinson
Hilary Forbes
Dean Beadle

And those who wished to remain anonymous.

I thank you all with all my heart. I could never have written this without you. I hope I have been faithful to your words and your school experiences, and that this book will help teachers for many years to come.

Thanks to Stephen, Sio and Matt, my wonderful family.

And to my English teacher, Mr Terry Morgan from 1981–1984, who believed I could be a writer.

INTRODUCTION

This book is for secondary subject teachers. The ones who are faithfully teaching a huge range of children day in, day out and having to navigate the pressures to get results, alongside the desire to instil a love of your subject to your pupils. We always hope we can do both, and I hope this book will make that more achievable when you have classes with autistic and neurodiverse children, who can be a great joy to teach.

Teachers are at the heart of any child's educational experience and the relationships we have with our pupils can impact them for the rest of their lives. Can you think back to something a teacher once said to you? Whether it was something negative, such as "You'll never make a runner" (once said to my husband who spent 20 years of his life doing fell running races and marathons), or something positive, such as "You would make a great teacher" (said to me by my English teacher when I was a painfully quiet and anxious 14-year-old).

In our daily classroom practice, we don't often get much time to reflect or to think differently about the way we teach or the individual needs and strengths of our pupils. And when we are forced to have to, it is often because there are behaviour or mental health issues that have caused a crisis. Most of the teachers I've ever met or worked with went into teaching to make a positive difference to children's lives and, despite the pressures and stress of the enormous daily demands, still want to invest in all pupil's lives.

So, what do we do when faced with a class that includes children who learn in ways that are different from how teachers typically teach? They may have a diagnosis or, more often, even

DOI: 10.4324/9781003280071-1

at secondary school, they are yet to be diagnosed. We can face different challenges, such as:

- Having multiple parental concerns.
- The challenges of having to show progress in learning for a child who may be struggling.
- Behavioural disruptions to our hours of carefully planned lessons and the effect that has on other children's learning.
- The data has flagged up a child who isn't engaging, who seems withdrawn.
- A pupil who struggles with relationships in the classroom and at breaktimes and that is evident in our lessons.

I also work with a lot of children who work hard to **mask** their difficulties in school, and the school thinks they are fine ... but their parents tell a different story.

The reality is that the way we teach and are taught to teach is often not the best way for autistic children to learn. Some of that is systematic, the way we organise our schools and the expectations put on secondary schools for results. This is often not conducive to inclusive education. The lack of training and dialogue about what inclusive education is in teacher training leaves many teachers ill equipped for the range of children they will be teaching in any subject. Inclusive education often brings to mind a classroom where children of all abilities and disabilities can be taught together and benefit from the social and cultural environment of understanding and learning together.

> The European Agency for Special Needs and Inclusive Education (EASNIE) (2018), has provided ample evidence that inclusive education increases social and academic opportunities for both children with and without disabilities, as well as significantly increases the likelihood that children with disabilities enrol in higher education and have better employment and life outcomes (see also Florian, Black-Hawkins and Rouse, 2017; Hehir, et al., 2016).
>
> *(Schuelka, 2018)*

This does demand that teachers are given the flexibility to adapt and reflect on the wide variety of needs and abilities of their students, year by year, and be supported and trusted to make their teaching fit the needs of their pupils. If we have school leaders and government agencies that understand this, then the whole approach to inclusion can be one where all children thrive. However, without focusing on all the barriers to this, which will depend on the country you are currently teaching in, there are approaches that all teachers can use to make school a positive and successful journey for autistic students, and other children with different Special Educational Needs and Disabilities (SEND), which is what this book is about.

I started out as a mainstream teacher in 1991 and majored in SEND education. After 14 years of teaching in schools I moved to a specialist school for autistic children, with a variety of learning difficulties, teaching all ages. Whilst there, I set up the school's outreach service. In 2014 I left to set up my own advisory service to mainstream schools, after seeing the huge need for support there. Now, some years later, I have a team of eight people, and five of us are specialist teachers. Some of our team are autistic, some are parents of autistic children and some have other neurodivergent conditions. I have worked with many secondary schools, seeing autistic and attention deficit hyperactivity disorder (ADHD) students through those critical five or seven years. I have helped many secondary-aged children go through the diagnostic process, Educational, Health and Care Plan (EHCP) applications and taught them about their autistic identity. I have trained Special Educational Needs Co-ordinators (SENCOs) and subject teachers, pastoral leaders and parents. In this time, I have learned the most from the autistic young people themselves. Giving them the means to tell us about what school is like for them has been the key to the success we have journeyed on together. From my pupils I have collected key information about what is difficult, what causes the most distress and what kind of support really helps in secondary school. I have listened to their journey through puberty, working out their identity, through the ups and downs of friendships, bullying, mental ill health, overcoming challenges and achieving (not just exam) success. I have seen so many autistic young people emerge from the end of secondary school and take the tentative steps into the next chapter of their lives. And I hope to share what I have learned with you in this book.

Throughout this book I will be giving you examples and quotes from children who have gone through the education system and have had support that enabled them to survive, and sometimes thrive. Autistic children are often very honest and direct, and given the space to communicate and someone with the time to listen, can give us important insights into what school is like for them and what can be done to make it better. Some autistic children struggle to find the words to communicate, and some may not be able to use spoken words as their communication language. The expectation to talk as evidence of learning in lessons can put them at a huge disadvantage. When I have worked with autistic children who are situationally mute, we have communicated quite adequately through writing, drawing or symbols. However, many autistic children who do not speak are assumed to have learning disabilities and are regularly sent to specialist schools where they are not always offered adequate communication tools. Naoki Higashida, who wrote *The Reason I Jump*, was given lessons on writing, and Jonathan Bryan, who wrote *Eye Can Write*, has a national campaign (Teach Us Too) to teach spelling and writing to non-verbal children. He has just finished his GCSEs. We don't know what intelligence autistic children have until we can connect with how they can communicate it. It is a common mistake to underestimate autistic children because their communication system is different to ours.

> *Please don't judge us from the outside only. I don't know why we can't talk properly. But it's not that we won't talk – it's that we can't talk and we're suffering because of it.*
>
> *(Naoki Higashida, 2014)*

When we have listened to our pupils, we are more able to put things in place that are right for them. The evidence plays out in a calmer and more engaged child, with more access to learning and development of better relationships. I am so looking forward to sharing their stories with you in this book.

I want to thank all the autistic children and adults who have contributed to this book. I believe passionately that we can change the school experience for so many other children by learning from their insights. I will be brutal and tell you that so many autistic students have been utterly failed by their educational experience, and many more have barely been able to survive. Many have ended up with mental ill health and trauma, and the damage has had a limiting effect on their lives into their adult years. But occasionally there is a spark of hope. And that hope comes from teachers, teaching assistants and pastoral staff like you who are reading this book. A teacher or teaching assistant, or even better, a head teacher and a whole school that 'gets' autism and works hard to make sure that autistic and other SEND children are given the best chance to thrive, no matter what it takes, saves lives. I have worked with schools that have changed small things that make a huge difference, and sometimes big things like school routines, systems and practices – for just one child. They have seen the benefit tenfold as other children they didn't realise needed that support started to thrive too. And that is what this book will help you do. Whether as a teacher or teaching assistant working on your own (I really hope you don't find yourself in this position, but it happens) or as part of a whole-school approach, what you do for your autistic pupils will never be forgotten by them. And I thank you for taking the time to investigate, understand and implement what they need. You are doing the right thing.

WHAT WE KNOW ABOUT AUTISM

Donna Williams, an autistic woman, wrote:

> *right from the start, from the time someone came up with the word 'autism', the condition has been judged from the outside, by its appearances, and not from the inside according to how it is experienced.*
>
> *(Donna Williams, 1996, p. 14)*

Throughout recent history, many people have been assuming autism is a set of observable behaviours. These might include rocking, flapping or lining up toys, and are invariably assumed to be seen more in boys than girls. For a long time, it was assumed autism was a childhood condition with the transition into adulthood largely ignored and much less planned for and supported.

We have come a long way from those outdated ideas of the 1940s, when Hans Asperger and Leo Kanner were studying boys with largely these stereotypical behaviours. In the 1980s, Lorna Wing and Judith Gould updated the diagnostic criteria and widened the understanding of autism, giving us a triad of impairments that were used as the standard diagnostic criteria until they were updated in the *Diagnostic and Statistical Manual* version 5 (DSM5) in 2013.

MYTH – AUTISM IS MORE COMMON IN BOYS THAN GIRLS

This is untrue – we used to have statistics that said for every one girl there were four boys identified as autistic. That was due to the outdated stereotyped behaviours that people thought were autism. Now we know more about the lived experiences of autistic people, we are catching up on identifying and diagnosing the girls we missed. It is likely that soon gender will be an irrelevant consideration or area for comment.

As Donna observed, however, diagnoses are still largely dependent on observable behaviours and many autistic young people, especially but not exclusively girls, are missed, misdiagnosed and deeply damaged by the lack of understanding and support throughout their education and home lives.

Although the 2013 revision of the DSM5 first included sensory processing difficulties, we are a long way from having those sensory differences explored beyond meeting the criteria for a diagnosis, even while autistic people are telling us how sensory processing is often at the heart of the many other difficulties they may have. We are still faced with a huge dilemma when it comes to identifying children, young people and adults who are autistic. The language of diagnosis is based on a medical model. This assumes that autism is the result of a deficit from what is considered to be 'normal.' Any assessment is based on what a person **cannot do and how they are significantly impaired by their condition**. The criteria uses such negative words as *abnormal, restricted* and *deficits*, which immediately negates the focus on what the child can do, what we can do to enable them and labels them as 'wrong,' 'broken' and 'abnormal.' This has seeped into our culture in schools. When we are given notice that a child has a diagnosis of autism, we can often jump to wrong conclusions or perspectives about what kind of student they are going to be and this can restrict our expectations of their potential.

> Autistic individuals are treated harshly for multiple reasons, primarily due to the language used to describe autism.
>
> *(Woods, 2017, page 61)*

The social model applied to autism sees the impairments people experience as largely caused by a lack of positive understanding, services and support. To reframe this in autism we may begin by seeing the 'deficits' as a difference, not a disorder. We still have a long way to go to flip this narrative, but I am going to convince you in this book that the place we can really make a difference is in schools. Teachers have the power to change the narrative around all areas of SEND and autism and to see the strengths and potential of autistic pupils. We can have good, strong ambitions for them and guide them to achieving that.

Labels and stereotypes are part of the problem. The current diagnostic label of Autistic Spectrum Disorder (or ASD) is based on the medical model. It implies deficit and negative outcomes. There are debates about 'levels' of autism and the disuse of the label 'Asperger's Syndrome.' In common language these are all a bit confusing for most people. As you read this book, you will see that every autistic child is different. Knowing this can help us understand some of the differences and uniqueness of each autistic child, so you can help them find the best way to achieve their potential without putting limits on what they might be able to achieve.

MYTH – WE ARE ALL A LITTLE BIT AUTISTIC

We are not. We are, however, all part of the human spectrum. To say this is to minimise the experience and challenges an autistic person has. One autistic friend says, "it's like saying you have backache and someone replying, 'we are all a little bit pregnant.'" Backache is clearly a common experience of being pregnant and many other conditions. In the same way, autism and other conditions are a set of strengths and difficulties identified by a distinct set of criteria. There may be common human experiences, but they are not all autistic at the root. All of these areas will be assessed and the autistic person will have differences in processing and living that are not the same as they are for a neurotypical person.

As my team of specialist teachers and I have studied autistic-led research and gathered the views and experiences of autistic children and adults, we have developed our own definition of autism based on what we have learned.

Autism is a different way of thinking and processing the world and the way senses take in information about the world. Autistic people might also process internal thoughts and sensations in a different way have strong passions and find security in repetitive behaviours. Autistic people are all different and most have many challenges when navigating the neurotypical world. The differences that autistic people usually have are in the

areas of communication, social experiences, sensory processing and the way they think and learn.

The Reachout ASC Team 2020

Even when we seek to be positive, there are debates about whether we say '**a person with autism**' or '**an autistic person**'. Once you listen to adults who have the diagnosis, you understand that **autistic** is the majority-preferred term. 'Disorder' means broken, not functioning as it should. This can do untold damage to the self-esteem of those receiving that diagnosis and impacts on the expectations others have of them. There is the same issue around using 'functioning' labels. Saying a child is 'high functioning' or 'low functioning' can lead to assumptions about the intelligence and capabilities of a child without testing these out, and dismisses the real needs of the autistic child who can manage academically and seems to manage verbally, but also leads to low expectations of the children who do not use speech or struggle to manage the sensory environment of a school (NAS, 2020).

We will use the term 'autistic' throughout the book whilst recognising that every autistic child or adult has the right to ask for the language that they prefer.

Neurodiversity is a term used to explain the diversity of human brains and how they function, acknowledging that human beings have a range of brain processing differences and need different environments to thrive. The term was coined by Judy Singer in 1999, and she advocated for neurodiversity to be recognised along with terms such as biodiversity in the natural world.

It is a developing term, which means the word is being applied and used by different people in different ways. It will take time to embed the term and how it is used in our language. There may always be differences of opinion on how it should be used. In this book, at this time, I am sharing what I understand is the affirming vocabulary of neuro-language.

Neurotypical is a term used to describe the dominant majority of neurotype, typically relating to the academic and social norms and expectations we have of children at certain developmental stages. Our education system is designed for neurotypical development.

Neurodivergent is a term used to describe the ways of thinking, processing and developing that are different from the neurotypical norms. It can include conditions such as autism, ADHD, dyslexia, dyscalculia, Developmental Coordination Disorder, Developmental Language Disorder, Tourette's Syndrome and some anxiety disorders as well as acquired brain injuries.

Please note that in this book we will be referring to autistic children. However, autism is a lifelong condition; it is the way someone IS and always will be. Please remember that our autistic children will be autistic adults, with potential to grow, to learn, to achieve, but they will always have their way of thinking, processing and experiencing the world. For this reason, you will see me refer to 'autistic people' interchangeably with 'autistic children' to remind the reader that these differences continue into adulthood. Our responsibility is not to make them 'pretend to be normal' as Donna Williams puts it, but to develop their autonomy and confidence as unique human beings.

CO-OCCURRING CONDITIONS

Brains are complex and awesome centres of processing, and autistic children can often be diagnosed with ADHD, dyslexia, epilepsy, dyspraxia, dyscalculia, Obsessive Compulsive Disorder (OCD), Developmental Coordination Disorder (formerly known as dyspraxia), Irlen Syndrome, Elhers-Danlos Syndrome, hypermobility, Developmental Language Disorder (DLD) or any other condition. There are more children with Down's Syndrome and Cerebral Palsy also being diagnosed as autistic. As teachers, this can seem overwhelming and leave us feeling ill-equipped to be specialists in all these conditions. The good news is that we don't have to be. The important thing to know when teaching an autistic or any other SEND child is to gather the information together and look at the bigger picture. Then, working with the child, the parent and with the school SENCO or leader for inclusion, set the priorities based on what the child can do, and what would help them most first. The important thing is to keep reviewing the impact and progress and keeping good records of this. Where children need more than the subject teachers can provide within their normal parameters of teaching (such as specific 1:1 adaptations or sensory support) then the teacher will need to seek help from their school SENCO or the SENCO may seek help from other agencies.

The most difficult aspect of providing any support in a secondary school is making sure that the support is consistent across all of the subjects and lessons in the school day. A child may have five different teachers, five different subjects and possibly five different support staff during one day. How we provide that consistency so that the child can access every subject and achieve their potential will be discussed and explored in this book.

MYTH – THERE IS AN EPIDEMIC OF OVER-DIAGNOSIS OF AUTISM

The truth is that we missed many of the girls and women who are autistic because we were not looking for them, and now we are. The other reality is that we have the internet and people are better informed, research is teaching us more about autism and autistic people are speaking up and sharing their lived experiences. So, a more-informed population is a better-diagnosed population. And we have yet to properly diagnose autistic people in some cultures and countries where they are not as yet well-informed. There is such a wide variety of autistic people and some will need a high level of support all their lives; some will need support in different ways because they can manage some things but not others; and some will need support only at particular times in their lives. It is important to know each individual so we can give them the support we can to enable them to thrive.

HOW I DO THINGS DIFFERENTLY

The voice of autistic children

COMMUNICATION

> *Communication between people with and without autism is a two-way problem. Individuals on the spectrum may have communication challenges to address, but their typical peers and conversation partners could do more to meet them halfway by accepting differences in the way they express themselves.*
>
> *(Spectrum News, accessed 15 February 2022)*

Communication is not just being able to talk. Psychologists believe that communication is made up of our words (7%), our tone and voice patterns (38%) and 55% comprises non-verbal cues such as body language, gestures, facial expressions (Mehrabian, 1967).

Autistic people all have communication skills, but the range and differences from the neurotypical expectations we have can be wide and varied, often unique to each autistic person. **There is a level of mutual understanding needed between two communication partners in order for the communication to be understood and successful. Misinterpretation can happen on any or both sides of the communication**. Therefore, when we are getting to know the communication of our autistic children, we have a lot of things to take into account. These are some of the first things to know and understand:

- Some autistic children only start to use verbal language late, and some use verbal language very early and have an extensive vocabulary. Autistic language development does not always follow a typical trajectory. Autistic children can

DOI: 10.4324/9781003280071-3

seem highly intelligent, but have gaps in their understanding of language or of certain social situations, and therefore struggle more than we realise. We have to be careful of assuming that their language ability means they understand everything that is said to them.

> *I learn phrases from soaps and American high school programmes so I can join in the conversations in my class. The other kids think I am just good at acting, and the truth is, I am, but it costs me a lot.*
>
> *(Autistic child, aged 14)*

- Some of the difficulties with language can be with the **syntax** (the way language is structured, such as grammar or the correct use of pronouns), but more often there is difficulty with the **pragmatics** (the way we use language socially and flexibly), the semantics (the meaning of words and phrases) or the **prosody** (the rhythm of speech – tone, inflection, etc.). Knowing these different aspects of communication through speech can help us understand the strengths and support needs of our autistic children.
- The non-verbal aspects of what is communicated, such as facial expressions and body language, might be difficult for autistic people to interpret. They may miss inferred meanings and take what is said literally. Autistic children can have a sense of humour that turns their logical and literal understanding into clever insights into non-autistic or 'neurotypical' people's language. Comedians such as Joe Wells or Hannah Gadsby are examples that I share with my students. Neurotypical people do not generally say what they mean, and autistic communication is generally more logical and honest.

Cullen (2018) stated:

> *Whilst it would be unreasonable to ask the Neurotypical (NT) population to stop using body language in the presence of [autistic] people, it would be greatly beneficial for*

both parties if the NT population also express verbally what they were trying to imply or express with nonverbal communication. This would mean both parties, NT and [Autistic] have a better chance of understanding each other.

- Autistic children often take longer to process what you have said. This can be because they are finding it hard to tune into your words (especially when there are other voices or background noise), because what you say has hidden meanings or assumptions that they are trying to work out, or because there are so many variables in their head that it takes time to figure out what exactly you are expecting from them.
- Processing time is so important for autistic children.

I'm always getting detentions for no reason. I'm just trying to do what I've been told but for some reason the teachers tell me I'm being rude or messing about. It's not fair when they don't explain things properly.

(Autistic child, aged 12)

Teachers talk too much. I try to work out what they were saying but they just keep talking over it and by the time I've worked out the first thing, there's been a million more instructions that I missed.

(Autistic child, aged 13)

- Visuals are often very helpful in supporting the communication of autistic children, especially our communication to them. A visual picture, diagram, list, infographic or sequence is a more permanent reminder, helps them understand the words better and can be more easily remembered when they need to recall the information. Those without verbal language (or those who are situationally mute) may need a visual communication system, such as writing notes or a laptop to type on, to provide them with their main means of communication.
- Ever since Temple Grandin, an autistic woman, described how she thought in pictures, it has been assumed that all

autistic people are more able to learn when a visual presentation of the communication is used. Whilst it is true, and has been reinforced by subsequent research, that many autistic people do respond better to visual communication, not all do, and so this needs to be checked out for the child in your class.

- Eye contact is often very challenging for autistic children and we should never insist that they look at us. For some, being able to look AND listen is difficult; for others, they feel actual pain when looking at someone else's eyes. Some autistic children seem OK with giving eye contact, but when you listen to their accounts, it is something they have learned to do to 'mask' their discomfort and try to fit in.
- It is easy for us to misinterpret the communication of autistic children. Their difficulty with prosody or direct honesty can sound like rudeness. Once we react to that without understanding the autistic child's intentions, we are in danger of discriminating against the child. Our cultural and racial biases need to be examined as we can misinterpret the autistic characteristics of, say, Black boys as aggression or oppositional behaviour instead of understanding their autism. There has been some excellent work done by Vanessa Bobb as she works to educate people about the cultural perspectives of autism in the Black and other ethnic communities (Bobb, 2019).

> *My children are Black. Yes, Black people can be autistic too! However, in our community, as with other cultural communities, there is a problem of under-diagnosis ... our voices are largely missing from research literature, conference and awareness-raising materials about autism.*
>
> *(Bobb, 2019)*

'STIMMING'

Self-stimulating or 'stimming' behaviours are an important part of what many autistic people say regulate their sensory and emotional states, as well as being a form of communication.

We might see or hear a child doing something repetitively and may try to stop them doing it, but please first ask yourself what harm they are doing. Self-stimulating behaviours are connected to sensory feedback and emotional regulation. The repetitive nature of behaviours such as rocking, flapping or fidgeting provide comfort and even joy. Most human beings 'stim.' Do you twiddle your hair or bite your fingernails? Do you flick a pen or tap your foot? All these things are the brain's way of calming down or alerting the person to be able to cope, pay attention or feel safe. Therefore, we should not try to 'get rid' of the stimming and not make a fuss about it in class, especially in front of other pupils. When the stim is harmful, such as biting themselves or picking at their skin, we should gently try to address the underlying stress and try to find a replacement activity that helps them feel safe and comforted.

Stims can be physical, sensory or verbal, and letting the child do what helps them regulate will be an important part of their support. In a secondary school there is the problem that differences are often picked on and made fun of by other children. Sadly, some of our autistic children say that they have been shouted at, given detentions and even made fun of by teachers when they have been stimming. It really is up to us to develop a culture in schools that is accepting and purposefully promotes acceptance of people in all their differences.

> *I hum when I am thinking because it shuts out all the distractions of the other kids talking and the road noise outside. I can't work any other way. My teachers either have to let me hum quietly or they get no work from me. Which do they want?*
>
> *(Autistic child, aged 15)*

> *I need to flap my arms at least twice a day. My school let me use a meeting room at break and lunch time so I could go and flap without anyone making fun of me. That made all the difference so I could go to my next lessons without feeling rubbish.*
>
> *(Autistic child, aged 12)*

If I don't move my body 'fizzes.' I can't concentrate, I can't do any work and I start to get easily annoyed by the other kids. Some of them start to tease me and wind me up when they see me getting fidgety. Some teachers tell me off. I act up because then I get sent out of the room and that brings relief ... at last I can move.

(Autistic child, aged 15)

Not everyone understands when I am self-stimulating. My way of doing this is by walking around the classroom which not all members of staff allow me to do. One in particular told me it was rude.

(Autistic child, Spectrum Gaming)

2

SOCIAL INTERACTION

All communication is social by its definition. What we often mean by social interaction is the making of friends and positive relationships, playing and doing activities together with mutual engagement and pleasure.

MYTH – AUTISTIC CHILDREN ARE ANTI-SOCIAL OR DON'T WANT FRIENDS

This is not true. Some autistic children withdraw from social situations because they are overwhelming (see Hilary's account below), they are too unstructured or the child has had negative experiences before that have destroyed their confidence. Most autistic children do want to have friends, but they want friends who will accept them for who they are, who will allow them to be themselves and who are kind. It's sad that this kind of friend is so elusive for so many autistic children and so many of them experience serious bullying.

When we say that autistic children have social difficulties it is often because we don't understand their experience of social situations. Dr Damian Milton (2018) has developed the Double Empathy Theory, which explains that whilst it is true that autistic people struggle to understand social cues, social meanings and what might be expected of them socially, it is also true that other people don't understand the social cues, social meanings and attempts at interaction from the autistic person's point of view. This can be incredibly useful for us teachers to understand

DOI: 10.4324/9781003280071-4

as we work to support autistic children, and you will see this theory threading through the advice we give.

> Dane wanted to be accepted by the other kids in his school. He wanted friends. But he also had poor eyesight and face-blindness so he couldn't recognise anyone. His solution in Year 9 (aged 14) was to try and make people laugh. He had heard some kids laughing when someone said a swear word in a silly voice, so he decided to copy that. He would go up to a crowd of kids, shout his silly swear word into the crowd and, if they laughed, would stay with them for the break trying to make them laugh. If they told him to go away (usually with more swearing) he would just go to the next group and try again.
>
> When I worked with him, he told me how lonely he was and that all he wanted was a friend who he could chat to at lunch times. At this point, his being autistic was not diagnosed so we got that sorted. Then I worked with him regularly to explore what he wanted and how he could recognise and approach people more successfully. We explored some lunch time clubs the school had, where he would meet the same people each week and we could explain to the others in the club that they would need to remind Dane of who they were so he could recognise them. This worked really well, and some months later, Dane told me about a particular friend he had made. Someone who accepted him, had the same sense of humour and had some shared interests.

Peter Vermueluen (2012) explains how the autistic brain functions in understanding the world, communication and interactions, and often finds pulling all the information together in its context quite difficult. The context of our communication impacts on what we are trying to communicate and what we understand from other people's communication to us. The difficulty for autistic children is that they may have a limited social library due to less (or negative) social experience, or that they take longer to find what they are needing in their memory and by the time they have worked it out, the context and situation have moved on and what they were going to do or say is no longer relevant. Even some autistic adults say that they often have no idea about what is going on in a social situation; they feel extremely vulnerable and anxious and suspect that other people are judging them unkindly. Autistic children are vulnerable to being taken advantage of by others who think it is fun to make the autistic child do things they shouldn't on the fake promise of being their friend. A lot of bullying can start this way and the danger for autistic children is that they may not know they are even being bullied until things get very seriously out of hand.

Unpredictability is a huge stress for many autistic children. It is why they like routine, order, to control things and to know exactly what is happening. Social situations, by their very nature, are full of unpredictable events, from not knowing what someone wants or what their mood is to where the conversation is going. Breaktimes and lunch times, when neurotypical children are usually relaxing and being refreshed for the next lesson, are not easy for many autistic children. Breaktimes are a cacophony of unpredictable noise, movement and social demands that cause huge amounts of stress. I urge you to observe and chat to your autistic child about breaktimes. Seeing it from their perspective is hugely valuable for our knowledge of how to support them.

> *My close, close friends understand because I've known them for a while, but apart from that I get called names on a daily basis and I can't tell anyone. I love my mum and dad and never want to stress them more than I already am.*
>
> *(Autistic child, Spectrum Gaming)*

ACCOUNT FROM AN AUTISTIC PERSON:

On a one to one, there is, well, one interaction. When another joins in then there are six potential interactions, because there is each person interacting with each of the other two so that is three interactions, plus each person's interaction with the other two, when the other two act as one in some way, e.g. opinion, agreement, etc. So 6 in total.

Now, there is an easy way to work out the number of interactions for a given number of people. If there are three people then we simply need to multiply 3 by 2 by 1 = 6. This is written as 3! The exclamation mark is known as a factorial sign. So then one more person joins...now there are 4! potential interactions which = 4 × 3 × 2 × 1 = 24. This may possibly be about my limit but mostly if I am one of the four people, but it's still a big challenge because now I am feeling all the unspoken undercurrents that 24 potential interactions produces. Throw into this several different personality types and possible tension between two or more of the people and it's possible to see how a storm can quickly brew of unspoken emotions, thoughts, etc.

However, I generally hang on in there, but know I'll pay the price with exhaustion and several recovery days where I avoid as much social interaction as possible. (Just a note to add that I do of course sometimes 'do' social groups with friends I know well or am comfortable with, as a trusted group of friends makes a huge difference, as does having a focus such as, having a meal with friends, and because I am already familiar with the types of interactions which happen and the whole experience is less exhausting. the better I know people in the group, the easier it is, generally. I still don't 'do' social events and social groups often though.)

Now, a fifth person comes along, and this basically explodes in my head. 5! potential interactions, that is 5 × 4 × 3 × 2 × 1 = 120 undercurrents which are cross-firing what is actually being said...add in a few looks, glances, smiles, frowns, tones of voice, buttings in, and there you have it, I'm gone, looking for the kettle and a quiet corner and maybe one person I know well enough to have a nice quiet brew with or better still friends' cat(s) who totally understand and retreated to quiet corners already. Add one more person...and now the potential number of interactions rises exponentially... 6! That's 6 × 5 × 4 × 3 × 2 × 1 = 720. 7 people, 7! = 7 × 720 = 5040 potential interactions.

What generally happens though, is that the limit of a useful group is probably four, though three is in my opinion better still. At 5, usually the quieter people give way to the more verbal, and melt into the background either gratefully or in some frustration. So this curbs the actual number of interactions, but not by much due to the unspoken emotions which flow like wifi among the group. I have come to realise that it must be an acute awareness of these ridiculous number of interactions, with equal awareness of the accompanying undercurrents that make the whole group experience feel to me as if I were being slapped in the face every nanosecond. The huge difference between a social group of say five people and a group which has gathered for a specific focus on say a film or lecture or even in some sense to play some sort of game or sport, is that if there is one focus that the group has then immediately it is in reality a one to one situation, almost, with each person in the group interacting mainly on the focus, and all 5 people also acting as one person interacting with the focus.

(Hilary Forbes, autistic maths teacher)

As Hilary pointed out, social interactions are often exhausting for autistic people. The effort and energy needed to manage in these situations take it out of them and there are often other stresses they are trying to manage whilst social situations are going on. Sensory differences have a huge impact, and we will look at those in more detail later in this volume. Some autistic children develop serious anxiety and mental ill health, because there are too many social demands and no rest from them.

Autistic burnout is a result. Sadly, this is becoming more common in younger teenagers and has been impacted by having time away from school (when life was quieter with fewer social demands) during the lockdowns of 2020, and returning to school afterwards. Many autistic children struggled to return to the social demands of regular school.

3

MASKING AND SPOON THEORY

There will be times in your teaching career, maybe as a form tutor, when you will hear from parents that their child is having meltdowns at home almost every day before or after school, and they will want to know what is happening at school to cause these. However, to your eyes, there will not be a problem at school. The child in your lessons seems a little quiet perhaps, but they are well behaved and have friends to hang around with at breaktimes. To you they are 'fine in school' and therefore it is easy to assume that the problem is that the parents are doing something wrong. This is a common problem for autistic children who have learned early on to **mask** their difficulties and autistic characteristics. It's more than just trying to fit in. It's often driven by huge anxiety and rejection sensitivity; this causes panic and trauma at the hint of getting anything wrong or being 'found out.' This **masking** becomes so second nature that it is not until you really study the nuances and details of their daily interactions that you realise that they are autistic. If undetected, this strategy can seem to be working, even as they start secondary school. But often it begins to unravel in the pre-teen years as the other children start to develop socially more complex relationships and the autistic child is left floundering. **Masking** is more than trying to fit in; it is a denial of their own identity and character, so much so that the autistic child is very vulnerable to disassociating from themselves and taking on the character and personality of others. Indeed, autistic children have been misdiagnosed with personality disorders because of this. The stress of holding this all in and keeping up the act at school all day becomes intolerable by the time the child reaches

DOI: 10.4324/9781003280071-5

their safe place at home. And then the emotional explosion happens.

Therefore, if a parent says their child is having meltdowns at home, please believe them and agree to investigate together. Imagine it like a bottle of cola that has been shaken up all through the day and the child has just managed not to let the lid blow off. But the lid will blow once the pressure has got too much. We can do a lot to ease that pressure gently throughout the day at school.

> *Safety is paramount for Autistic people and Masking makes up a huge part of keeping safe and that's where our 'umbrella' definition comes in, because Masking is what we do to keep us safe, Autistic Masking is the act of an Autistic person presenting themselves as a non-Autistic person... Masking is a build up of layer upon layer of mass complexity, whereby an Autistic person attempts to 'fit in' and maintain safety in an endless variety of differing situations and environments by applying in fluctuating degrees often uncontextualised and sometimes rehearsed, learnt behaviours to appropriate situations; whilst simultaneously suppressing natural behaviours and conjunctively their sense of self-identity, initially consciously, over time becoming unconscious, often at great cost.*
>
> *(Kieran Rose, 2021)*

SPOON THEORY[1]

Ann Memmott, who blogs at www.annsautismblog.co.uk, first introduced me to the Spoon Theory in relation to autism. It was originally created by Christine Miserandino when asked about her chronic illness (you can read the original post here: www.butyoudontlooksick.com/articles/written-by-christine/the-spoon-theory/), but is a great way of helping us understand why school and college is such hard work for autistic children and young people.

Let's imagine that the social, sensory and intellectual energy an autistic person has each day can be measured in '**spoons**.'

An autistic person can start the school day with a full drawer (which may be only half as full as that of a typical child), or with some of their spoons already used up in dealing with the demands of getting there. Depending on various factors such as whether they slept, if their family remembered to say goodbye the right way, if their clothes are itching their skin, if their routine was changed or any number of other seemingly incidental events, they may be starting the day with, say, only 20 spoons instead of 30.

Then they need to start using their **spoons**. Each set of instructions, each set of work demands, each time they have to organise themselves, each change of classroom, each new subject, every time they follow a complex set of instructions or cope with change and each social interaction may cost the autistic person a **spoon**. If there are sensory sensations that are overwhelming, then another **spoon** is used up in regulating and keeping calm. If they have to work in a group more than one **spoon** may be needed. Breaktimes are not relaxing - another **spoon** or two is used up in coping with all the social interaction, noise and lack of structure. Some manage to save a **spoon** by shutting off, taking the time to be alone, so that they can cope with the next set of lessons.

I hope you can see what might be happening. You have a child or young person who seems OK in the morning but always seems to lose it in the afternoon. Or they won't join in anything at breaktimes and pace around the perimeter of the yard or social space. Or they have meltdowns some days but are fine on other days. Or parents ask you what you are doing to their child as they always have a meltdown as soon as they come out of school ... and getting them to do homework is impossible. You may have a child who seems not to be able to speak to you on some days, is unable to socialise and seems distracted and distressed.

You might assume you need more structure in the afternoons. You might assume you need to teach the person some social skills so they can make friends at breaktimes. You might assume the parent isn't disciplined enough. You might put all kinds of practical support in place, but it doesn't really work.

It may just be that the autistic child has **used up all their spoons**. They have no communication, organisation, sensory, social or intellectual energy left. They might just be able to keep it together at the beginning of the week, but then are far too exhausted to carry on by Wednesday. Some days there may be no spoons to deal with the things they usually seem OK with. They might even be able to keep it together through the day but cannot regulate themselves in the safety of their home. Some even manage to **borrow spoons** from the next day but there will be a day when there are no spoons left to borrow and the person has a major meltdown. Autistic children can crash out of school with burnout without us seeing their **spoons depleting**. How can you, when you only see them for an hour each week? It really does need a more joined-up approach to collating what all teachers notice. The advice in this book covers many of the ways you can support to conserve and maximise **spoons** in the autistic children you teach.

NOTE

1 Taken from my blog, https://reachoutasc.com/spoon-theory-and-autism/.

THE AUTISTIC SENSORY EXPERIENCE

All the information we take in about the world around us comes in via our senses.

Sensory processing is the brain's act of taking in the sensory information, putting the bits that fit together to make sense of a situation and making meaning out of what is happening. This is really important for everyday activity. From getting out of bed to going to sleep, your brain is constantly taking in and assessing sensory information. We cannot function without our brains knowing what is going on, sending messages to our muscles and joints to make us move, to avoid things that are dangerous or uncertain and to manage self-care and keep safe. We mostly do all these things without thinking. We don't think about how to walk once we have mastered the skill as a child, our brain develops its motor memory and we just walk. However, it's much more complex than that as you can imagine, and there is no space in this book to go into greater detail. **But what we need to know as teachers is that the sensory processing of our autistic pupils is fundamental to everything else ... Their access to everyday environments, their communication, their social interactions, their emotions and their thinking and learning**.

Autistic people are telling us that the sensory experiences they have are largely dependent on the environments we have created and also the internal sensations and motivations they have. Therefore, some environments are overwhelming and sensory 'hell' for autistic children, and many behaviours we see are the autistic person either trying to cope with the sensory

DOI: 10.4324/9781003280071-6

'hell' or a way of seeking sensory comfort and regulation internally. There is increasing evidence that autistic people suffer from sensory trauma and this can lead to long-term difficulties with mental health the longer it goes on. Making our environments more accessible for autistic children becomes essential, because to not do so is abusive. But the environment is not just the classroom and the things we have on the wall, but the expectations, demands, unpredictability and interactions that are expected of people. All of this piles on the pressure for an autistic child who processes or interacts with the world differently from their neurotypical peers.

We must remember that **sensory joy** is a thing too, and that a child's interests, certain movements in PE, the light coming through a prism, cooking smells or textures in DT can create joyful moments that are intense and wonderful. If this is something in your lesson, then let them enjoy that. It is something we should feel privileged to have created or allowed.

The reality for our autistic children in school is that the environment, the lessons and all the demands of the day can be perceived differently through their senses. They may have a much smaller 'window of tolerance' in some sensory systems than other children which will impact on the energy and effort they need just to manage that, and this can cause them pain and distress throughout the day. The sensory systems can be a mixture of over- and under-sensitive in any child, and environmental conditions, anxiety and tiredness can further complicate the situation; e.g., not just increase sensitivity, but also make processing information more challenging. It is not uncommon for the sensitivity to change throughout the day. For example, when a child might be tired in the afternoon.

> *I can tell you the name and model of every aeroplane that flies over our school because I know the different engine sounds. Being in a classroom is like torture. I can hear absolutely everything in my classroom and the three classrooms around us. I spend the whole lesson trying to concentrate on the teacher's voice and it is exhausting. I am always anxious about what the other kids are going to*

do or say, which means I am fighting that too. I go home and I have to go to bed, with my earphones in to recover. The thing is, that listening to music helps. But the teacher said I can't listen to music in class.

(Autistic pupil, aged 16)

It will help us to understand that there are eight sensory systems.

- These can all be **hypo-**, or **under-sensitive**, which means that the brain does not receive enough sensory feedback or stimulation and may either ignore or seek out more sensory input. This can be seen in children who are constantly seeking movement, for example. Often it is much less noticeable, such as when a child doesn't respond to someone talking to them or seems to be zoning out of what is going on around them.
- Alternatively, the sensory systems can be **hyper-**, or **over-sensitive**, which means that the brain is receiving too much information and finds it hard to cope or manage it. This can be seen when children put their fingers in their ears, or refuse to go into a room that might smell bad to them, or have huge anxiety and fear in the school and home environment. It can be caused by anything from clothing to noise and smells. The school environment is a place of overwhelming sensory experiences.
- Some autistic children experience synesthesia, which is a neurological condition in which information meant to stimulate one of the senses stimulates several or a different one of the senses. For example, it may be that they can taste people's names or see numbers as colours.

This is a general overview of some of the sensory processing experiences we can find in autistic children.

1. **Sight** – the visual system includes what we see and how we interpret all the parts of what we see to make a whole picture. Our brains interpret the sights and put them together

with the other relevant sensory signals (such as sounds) to help us interpret the world around us.

- In school, autistic children may have difficulty using their sight to follow and track our teaching from the whiteboard or to read and write and they could have dyslexia.
- Autistic children can be face-blind (a small percentage but worth checking), colour-blind, have Irlen Syndrome (requiring coloured lenses to see clearly) or fractured visual perception.
- They may only be able to focus on certain narrow or specific details or be easily distracted by the huge amounts of movement, displays, colours, light levels and visual changes in school.
- They may have an excellent visual memory that helps them learn, and be a strong visual learner.

Walking down the corridors was difficult for Harriet because her visual sensory perception was distorted by the similar-coloured walls and floor. She couldn't see her route through the corridors, and could only manage to walk around school by holding onto the walls and staring at the join between the wall and the floor. Stairs were easier because there was a darker strip on the edge which made the stairs easily distinguishable. It helped her when she was allowed to leave her lessons a few minutes before everyone else and navigate the corridors when they were quiet.

Teachers used to get annoyed with me when I didn't make eye contact. They also denied me leaving the class and I was really overwhelmed so I just walked out of class, and I got detention.

(Autistic child, Spectrum Gaming)

2. **Hearing - autistic children are often very sensitive to sound.** Most of the autistic children we support in secondary

schools have issues with the daily noise. Sometimes it is specific noises, and sometimes it is the general level of background noise.

- They can find it difficult to distinguish different tones of sound, distinguish different voices or filter out background noise.
- For some, sound feels like bullets in their head and can give them pain. This is also known as hyperacusis.
- As Hilary explained earlier, the more voices there are to switch attention to, the harder it is to manage conversations and tune into what is important to them.
- I have known schools that allow autistic pupils to listen to music, or wear noise-cancelling headphones. Their approach to making school fair for everyone was that everyone needs what they need to thrive and that might be different for everyone. You **can** do that in your own lessons.
- Some autistic children can have coexisting auditory processing disorder which means they will struggle to process the instructions and verbal teaching you give to the class. Some can be helped with personal listening devices, noise-cancelling headphones or apps that record and replay speech.

> *All through my lessons I was anxious about when the bell was going to go off as the noise made my brain explode. Five times a day, every day.*
>
> *(Autistic child, aged 12)*

> *I just wanted the classrooms to be quiet, but no matter how much the teacher tried to keep everyone silent it wouldn't be enough. I could hear the surrounding classes talking. It was hell. That was enough to make me ill.*
>
> *(Autistic child, aged 12)*

3. **Smell** – the sensitivity to smell can be heightened in an environment where there are many people and where food is being served. We can underestimate the number of

smells in a classroom. Many of us desensitise to familiar smells but many autistic children may not.

- The food being cooked in the kitchen, your perfume or the sweaty bodies of children after PE can cause a lot of distress and lead to an autistic child doing all they can to avoid certain areas or lessons.
- The school toilet smells can be particularly overwhelming and distressing for autistic children (noise, bright reflections and crowds can affect this too). This can lead to infections and illness when they are unable to use the toilet all through the school day.
- Other autistic children may have a poor sense of smell and cannot tell when they have body odour or when something is burning, for example. This can also impact on the range of foods that they will eat.
- Some may seek out strong smells and enjoy strong flavours, and some may be constantly chewing as taste and smell are so connected.

> I once had a child say to me "I can't work with you today, you stink." And I realised that I had put perfumed deodorant on that day. He was right and we managed to sit far enough apart for that visit to manage the session I had come to do. But I remembered to wear my unperfumed deodorant every time after that.

4. **Taste** – our sensation of taste is connected to our sense of smell and touch, and is not just about food. Think about the taste of toothpaste, for example.
   - School breaks and lunch times can be so overwhelming for autistic children. Other people eating, the range of choices of food, the smells and the pressure to try new things can all induce sensory stress. Other children may eat a lot and find sensory comfort in food.
   - They may have a limited palate of foods they can manage to eat without it making their senses scream, or

they may have the need to control the order and pace at which they eat.

- For some, eating in front of others in the noisy hall and the demands to hurry up or eat something in a different order can be very distressing. This shows how our sensory systems interact with each other.
- We need to be aware that eating disorders can develop in autistic children through sensory intolerances, sensory seeking needs and needing to control their environment or what goes into their body.
- Be aware of this in food technology lessons. Autistic children may need some adaptations, such as being able to sit near an open window or near the door. They may need to be able to cook something that is tolerable to them, and not be made to cook something that assaults their senses.
- For information about autism and eating disorders there are links in the Resources chapter.
- Some autistic children have a strong need to be chewing as a sensory regulation strategy They will chew anything from a pen top to their sleeves and if it is possible to allow them to chew gum or a descrete piece of 'chewelry' (such as a silicone-type bracelet they can wear under their shirt sleeve) this could help them feel regulated in class.

When foods are touching or mixed like in a sauce I gag so much I cannot eat anything else at all. I need my foods to be familiar and apart from each other. I wish people would leave me alone when I'm eating too.

(Autistic child, aged 13)

5. **Touch - our skin is our main touch organ and light touch is different from firm touch**. The over-sensitivity or under-sensitivity to touch can impact on any lessons, and an autistic child's interactions with others. It could be they need to touch things around them to understand those things fully.

- Autistic children often hate the unpredictability of people being near them, or being in crowds (or lining up!) because they might touch them, and the lack of control on top of the horrible sensation is terrifying.
- Some autistic children can't stand touching certain textures, or textures that are mixed together. Some can't stand the labels on clothing or the seam in their socks, or wearing shoes.
- Touch sensitivity can impact on subjects such as science, DT and PE. The texture of equipment and objects needed for doing practical activities may be intolerable for an autistic child. Again, flexibility will help. If a child is having a problem, give the objects to another child and let them watch, substitute them for something more tolerable or do it with them as the class demonstration.
- Some autistic children seek out touch, wanting to hug people or stroke lots of things in the classroom. They may have favourite cuddly toys or a piece of fabric they need for sensory comfort, even bringing it to secondary school with them.
- Some develop a fear of touching things, or a need to do repetitive actions that help them ground themselves in an intolerable environment.

School uniform is often a sensory problem for many autistic children, and I am convinced that a more flexible approach would benefit so many children. Imagine going to work in a scratchy sack and having to sit in it all day. You could choose to leave and find another job. Children have to go to school and are punished for not being able to tolerate the torturous clothing.

(Autistic teacher)

Overall, the teachers and support staff could not have been nicer; they all had copies of my support plan, which highlighted how my Autism affected me. If they saw me struggling or upset, they would ask if I wanted to go to the respite room or if there was anything they could do to help. For example, my art teacher let me wear plastic gloves when handling paint or clay, as I did not like the texture.

(Jackson, aged 21, reflecting on his secondary school experience)

6. **Vestibular (balance) - this is our sense of movement and balance**. The vestibular sense is important for coordination and organisation. We use it to support our tracking, e.g., looking up from a desk to the board and back again. It tells us if we are moving, whether that is fast or slow, up or down, in a straight line or in different directions and helps us keep our balance when our body is in a precarious position.
   - Autistic children may have poor balance and struggle with planning the speed and coordination of movements.
   - They may be over-sensitive and have motion sickness, that they may not be able to explain to you (it is perhaps just their normal state) which will impact on the way they move around the classroom and school, and make PE very challenging.
   - They may have excellent balance and love to climb and move at every opportunity.
   - Some autistic children may seek out movement to calm an overstimulated sense - which may include rocking on their chair, getting up out of their seat and fiddling with objects in your lessons. This is 'stimming,' and no amount of telling off or asking them to stop will make the need go away. A child might become more disruptive or internalise their distress and that is not good for them. Instead, find ways to help them move. It could be giving out books, collecting something from the staffroom or even letting them walk around at the back of your lesson whilst you talk to the class. I have known a teacher provide a standing desk for a child which was a huge success.

7. **Proprioception - this is our body and spatial awareness.** People don't have over-sensitive proprioception sensory systems, but this sensory system can be under-sensitive. Some autistic children are very good at sports and coordinated movements. This body awareness is centred in your muscles and joints, giving the brain feedback as to where you are, planning movements and reactions.
   - Dyspraxia, or Developmental Coordination Disorder (DCD) as it is now called, is closely related to poor proprioception.
   - An autistic child may be very fidgety, unable to regulate their body to stay still comfortably. The brain is just not receiving enough feedback and sends strong requests for more movement so it can register where the body is and if it is safe.
   - They may be sluggish, always leaning on walls and people to feel grounded and find it difficult to manage in their own space.
   - Autistic children with under-sensitive proprioception may need support in their seating, movement breaks to develop body awareness and need to 'stim' to gain the feedback from their body that the brain needs.
   - Anxiety and concentration have been proved to be improved by proprioceptive exercises or activities.
   - Fiddling, doodling and 'stimming' are self-regulating activities that actually help autistic children listen better, and this is probably true for children with attention deficit hyperactivity disorder (ADHD) too. You can build in some boundaries and rules, such as it has to not impact on others (yes, I have had children flicking their elastic bands at others too!). Have blue tack or hair bands available to fiddle with, talk about them with your class and let it just be a normal way of working. I can tell you that as an adult I constantly need to use a fiddle object in order to concentrate on someone talking in a meeting. If it is hard for adults, then let's help children find their way to regulate that optimises their learning.

PE should have more options. For those who are not sporty (or who hate team sports at least) and who are not well co-ordinated, we should be able to do things that allow us to build strength and coordination for ourselves, not to be part of a team.

(Autistic child, aged 14)

8. **Interoception is our awareness of internal sensations** - this is one of the most important breakthroughs in our understanding of the sensory systems. Interoception regulates our internal sensations like knowing when we need to go to the toilet, when we are hungry, feeling pain, sickness, tiredness and the like.
   - For girls, periods can either be difficult to register or be overwhelmingly painful.
   - Some autistic children struggle to receive the messages from their bodies that they are hungry, or need the toilet and can still have wet accidents whilst in secondary school.
   - Others can be over-sensitive and constantly feel like they need to eat or go to the toilet, can feel pain more intensely than is usual and have huge reactions to others being hurt, even on videos. This is something like pain synaesthesia, where the person feels pain or discomfort in the same area that they see others being hurt.
   - Interoception is also connected to our emotions and our ability to recognise when we are feeling an emotion. Emotions are complex events. Thoughts, body sensations and reactions (such as flight, fight or freeze) are felt internally, and some autistic children do not always register or recognise those messages from the body in the conscious brain (and therefore communicate how they are feeling). We call this alexithymia.
   - Alternatively, some autistic children are hyper-sensitive to emotions. This means they feel them in their bodies as huge reactions. Sadly, they are often dismissed as over-reacting, and in the puberty years, emotions are affected by hormones which can heighten the anxiety

> they feel, often leading to self-harming and suicidal ideation.

As a subject teacher you can work on having a calm classroom and looking out for those small adaptations that could make all the difference to the autistic children you teach. Anything from letting them go early to lunch, to allowing them to fiddle or doodle while they are listening will make a difference and will be appreciated by them for many years to come. There is a strong link between sensory soothing and managing anxiety, so we must be very careful not to stop or dismiss an autistic child's rocking, fiddling or doodling, for example. Being told to stop and made to feel wrong (or so fearful in class in case they are told off) does not make an autistic child feel 'normal.' It internalises their distress and causes long-term anxiety and mental ill health (Verhulst et al., 2022).

I do a lot of small group and 1:1 work with autistic children in secondary schools and the most common topics we cover are sensory reactions and emotional regulation. Finding a way to help them communicate their emotions comes first, and we have used colours, shapes and characters if the regular emotion words don't mean anything to them. As a subject teacher, asking an autistic child how they are feeling may not elicit a response, and is unlikely to give you an accurate picture. If you can, build a communication code between you and the child that can help them tell you when they are struggling or are OK. If we take the baseline as being 'OK' or 'calm,' then even a 3-point scale from that can give the child an easier way to ask for help or respite.

1	2	3
Calm/OK	Struggling/anxious	Terrible/not coping

All autistic children are unique in how their sensory systems work and function, and an individual approach can be supported in a mainstream classroom.

TEACHING AUTISTIC CHILDREN

Practical strategies

5

GETTING IT RIGHT FROM THE START

YEAR 7S (11–12 YEARS OLD)

Starting secondary school is often a more challenging adjustment for autistic children. One of the hardest things to get used to is having different teachers in different classrooms and the pace of changing between one and the next. Helping all your Year 7s settle in will be part of your job and I am sure you have some good tips and tricks that help them in those first few weeks. Autistic children often take longer to settle, however. In the schools I work with, we monitor the autistic children for far longer than the other children. Social challenges, sensory challenges, as well as huge stress from having to do homework often cause a lot of stress and anxiety.

- If you are a form tutor, it would help if you can connect with the autistic children in your form through their interests and have a regular daily or weekly check-in with them.
- In subject lessons, pass on any concerns, especially about their mental health, however small, to the Special Educational Needs Co-ordinator (SENCO) or head of year so they can be monitored. One thing that our autistic children always comment on are the teachers who take the time to get to know them, give them some say in where they sit and take the time to explain things properly.
- You could film a video or send an email to their home before they start in September to remind them of who you are, reassure them you are there to help and include a schedule of what will happen on the first day.
- If you have a timetable of form time topics (some schools do PSHE in this time), have it displayed on the wall. If there

DOI: 10.4324/9781003280071-8

are messages, give the children time to jot down some notes and have the week's messages displayed on a board in your room.

- Take the time to speak to parents so that they know who you are and how they can contact you. Tell them the expected time it might take to reply because of your teaching commitments and who to contact if there is something urgent.
- Some autistic children benefit from a school-to-home notebook/diary to relay information, such as if the child has had a tough weekend or if they need a reminder to bring some equipment to school. Often the management of this will fall to a teaching assistant (TA) – but work with them to pass the information on.

> *In my current school I talked to my teachers about not wanting to be around people. They understood and tried to help me not have to have my personal space invaded but not be isolated for the duration of the entire term.*
>
> *(Autistic child, Spectrum Gaming)*

RULES AND EXPECTATIONS, DISCIPLINE

The rules and sanctions in a secondary school are often strict and complex after the environment of a primary school. With the best support, secondary school teachers can be consistent, but the reality is that each teacher will apply sanctions and rewards in their own way. This can make an autistic child highly anxious. I have known autistic children come to crisis point over the fear of getting a sanction, and many more who don't understand why they are getting sanctions for asking for help or being accused of not listening when the reality is that they don't understand what you said. A no-excuses policy in any school is highly damaging to autistic children, and when they are punished for seeking sensory regulation (such as fidgeting in class, walking around school with a hood over their head, undoing their top button), they are in danger of discrimination. The question I get asked a lot is, "What about the other children?" We really need to take charge of this and not use it as an excuse to torture autistic children, trying to make them manage the same as everyone else who has different needs. Reasonable adjustments as laid out in law (Equality Act, 2010) apply to children too and disability is one of the protected characteristics. We can make adjustments, and yes, other children may challenge that, but they are teenagers and that's what they do. A clear policy and consistent approach that allows for adaptations should be the norm in all schools. The issues it creates can be addressed by the senior leadership, in PSHE and Citizen lessons and by reflecting on what enables all children to thrive in your school.

Ideally a whole-school approach will discuss difference, exploitation, disability, ability and equality of opportunity and share stories from people of different cultures, sexualities and disabilities. You could invite autistic adult speakers to share their stories and have an agreed common reply to 'it's not fair' that all teachers can reinforce.

The UK Government's paper *Behaviour in Schools Advice for Headteachers and School Staff* (2022) mentions that reasonable adjustments should be made for children with Special Educational Needs and Disabilities (SEND).

How that looks in your lessons would be to consider the following:

- For autistic children, behaviour is often a form of communication. *"I wish that they knew that I don't always feel comfortable talking about how I feel because I don't have the courage to ask for help most of the time"* (Autistic child, Spectrum Gaming). If you can pause and ask, "what is difficult for them in this lesson?" you are more likely to be able to support them.
- A quiet reminder of what you do want is more effective than telling a child off in front of the class and just telling them to stop doing a behaviour.
- If a behaviour is unsafe, explain clearly why you are unable to allow them to continue doing that and offer an alternative or a way out.
- If the child has a time out card, they may feel unable to use it out of fear of comments or getting into trouble. If you notice

they seem uncomfortable or anxious, ask them if they would like a break, or to go and work in a quieter place with the TA.

- Ask the child why something is a problem for them. Offer to speak to them at breaktime. Or you could ask them to write down why there is a problem. I know you don't often have time in the lesson to follow this up. If you can't meet with the child afterwards, write them a note to reassure them you listened. It is OK to say why you did what you did, or why they needed to do something different.
- Be able to say sorry.
- Pause, distract them by reminding them what they can do, use humour and redirect their attention as your first response.
- There is a difference between responding and reacting. When we react it is often out of emotion, frustration, anger, tiredness or feeling out of control. Read some good alternative books on behaviour such as those by Paul Dix. Responding is more considered and enables us to stay in control of a situation.

> As part of meeting any of these duties, schools should, as far as possible, anticipate likely triggers of misbehaviour and put in place support to prevent these. Illustrative examples of preventative measures include (but are not limited to):
>
> - short, planned movement breaks for a pupil whose SEND means that they find it difficult to sit still for long;
> - adjusting seating plans to allow a pupil with visual or hearing impairment to sit in sight of the teacher;
> - adjusting uniform requirements for a pupil with sensory issues or who has severe eczema;
> - training for staff in understanding conditions such as autism.
>
> Any preventative measure should take into account the specific circumstances and requirements of the pupil concerned.
>
> *(Section 38, p. 17,* Behaviour in Schools Advice for Headteachers and School Staff, *September 2022)*

WORKING WITH PARENTS

Right from the beginning of Year 7 the relationship and communication with parents need to be on solid ground. Parents have a wealth of experience and knowledge, not just about their child but of the SEND system and about autism. I have worked with parents just setting out on the journey of getting their child identified and diagnosed, to those who have a Master's degree in Autism, run a local support group for families and are a wealth of information. When there are a lot of different teachers and subjects, there could be a need to talk to you about how the child is doing in your subject specifically and a greater need to explain homework to parents so that they can help their child complete it. One of the best things you can do is communicate positive achievements to parents. Having that battle with the SEND system, trying to get help so that their child can get into school and achieve their potential is exhausting. Knowing there are teachers who understand and see the positives in their child means such a lot.

> *Getting that postcard from the History teacher telling me my daughter was a joy to teach and how he loved her wealth of curious facts that she told him in class lifted the whole family. Never underestimate the power of a positive word.*
>
> *(Parent of autistic 13-year-old)*

In their book *Championing Your Autistic Teen at Secondary School* (2022), Gareth Morewood and Debby Elley suggest giving autistic students a one-page outline of key people to communicate with and what they can go to them about. This is a great way of helping autistic children learn about their support networks. I would add to this that:

- A form tutor can go through this with the autistic child at the beginning of the year and make sure that parents have a copy they can reinforce at home. Be clear about why they have a TA, your role as their form tutor and who their pastoral lead is.

- You may have a chaplain, librarian or school nurse that would be a safe person for the autistic child to go and talk to about things that worry them. Be aware that you can set all this up and the autistic child will still find it difficult to ask for help, but we can build a regular meeting with a key person, checking in with them and using good communication that doesn't pressure them.
- We also need to ask specific questions. For example, if we keep asking, "are you OK?" they are more than likely to say "yes," because the question is too wide, and too much could be going on inside their heads to focus on anything specific to say. They may be in a rush, or have no **spoons** left to get into a conversation. You might have asked it in front of others and they don't want others to know. It is better to make an appointment, and ask specific questions like "are you managing to keep up with your homework in maths?" Or "what's the hardest thing about lunch times for you?"

Gavin is situationally mute in school. He rarely talks but then tells his parents how stressed and anxious he is about school when he gets home. His mental health has deteriorated but he wouldn't speak to anyone at school about it. The SENCO set up a daily meeting at morning break with the school chaplain who had a nice, calm and quiet room. They communicated through writing notes on Post-It notes and put them into a book. The chaplain would report back on anything she could deal with or pass on to a teacher to sort out and they could look back at what had been achieved over the year.

6

QUICK WINS FOR TEACHING AUTISTIC CHILDREN

In my years of working with secondary schools I have had the privilege of sitting in and observing a wide variety of lessons. I have noticed lots of teaching strategies that work well for autistic and neurodivergent children, and lots of teaching strategies that don't. I thought it would be useful to make a list of what counts as good teaching for autistic children.

GETTING TO KNOW PUPILS

- The teacher has a relationship with the autistic child and treats them with a friendly manner.
- The teacher is curious about how they can help all children.
- Teachers who really love their subject and share their passion whilst sharing links to what is relevant to the children.
- Teachers who don't make fun of or pick out the autistic child in public when they need redirecting. They speak to them one to one, and in a low, calm voice.
- Teachers that give careful thought to the seating arrangements that help the autistic children first. They ask the children where they want to sit.
- Teachers that are aware of the quiet and studious autistic children and what helps them in their lessons.
- Teachers understand that they are not 'doing it on purpose' - autism is a difference, and school is much harder work, even when they try so hard.

DOI: 10.4324/9781003280071-9

LESSON STRUCTURE

- Teachers who use visuals on the whiteboard to introduce a clear point to the lesson.
- They show and explain to the whole class how the lesson will be structured.
- They organise the lesson in chunks with a clear structure to each part.
- If there are multiple instructions, they are written down so the children can check where they are up to.
- When teaching, they underline keywords in instructions; for example, <u>similarities</u> and <u>differences</u>.
- For those autistic children who struggle to copy off the board, they give out a printed copy of the text and give the children time to read and understand it, while the rest of the class are copying.
- They cue the student into the lesson. "Good morning and welcome to Geography. Today we will be ... " can make all the difference.
- They structure group work, and give each person in the group a specific task, written down. Pairs work better than groups. (But working on their own might produce better work for some.)
- They allow for and manage sensory and movement breaks. Autistic children have very good reasons for struggling to sit for long periods of time.

ENSURING LEARNING HAPPENS

- A teacher who uses a silent starter that is accessible and explains how it links to what they did before, and when they did it.
- The teacher pauses occasionally to give thinking, processing or doing time.
- The teacher gives one clear instruction and then doesn't talk over the pupils while they do it.
- When questions are asked of the class, pupils write notes or bullet points so they can remember those key points in their main task. (Sometimes a teaching assistant (TA) will do this for a SEND child but for the same reason.)

- When using video, the teacher pauses to ask questions and allows the students to write notes before moving on to the next part.
- Teachers who say what they mean, explain what revision is (and how it helps) and give a balanced context to exams.
- A teacher who challenges and extends those autistic children who find the work easy.
- Homework support. A teacher who considers quality over quantity and adapts homework. They use familiar, repetitive and highly structured tasks wherever possible. They make adaptations when homework is just not possible for the child.

> *What a breakthrough at school! They finally understood that my panic at getting anything wrong on paper is a very real thing, and have let me use my iPad instead - this means that if I make a mistake, I can digitally erase it and the panic goes away at once. Before then I had my mistake staring at me, and I had to live with the knowledge that there was nothing I could do about it.*
>
> *Zane (*Avoiding Anxiety in Autistic Children, *Dr Luke Beardon, p. 31)*

There are some things to definitely avoid. These strategies often cause stress to the autistic children, make them anxious and lead to what I call "verbal combat" where the teacher and child are both stressed and arguing and the child ends up being disciplined for something that could have easily been avoided. Sometimes it leads to the autistic child shutting down, head on the table and unable to continue working. Others may seem OK, but the build-up leads to anxiety and self-harm or other mental ill health.

- Blaming autistic children for not listening when they couldn't keep up with your verbal input.
- Insisting an autistic child 'looks at you' when you are talking to them. **Please understand that this is often incredibly uncomfortable or painful and they are not being rude**.

- Giving a distracted or disruptive pupil more sanctions than anyone else. This might like seem you are stamping down on it before they take it too far, but it rarely helps and can be interpreted as bullying the child.
- Arguing with an autistic child who has actually told you a truth. Feeling like they have challenged your authority rather than admitting your humanity.
- Trying to engage a child in conversation when they are in the middle of a task. They are concentrating and don't need to be distracted.
- Threatening the child with detentions or other punishments when they are overloaded and shutting down.
- Telling children that GCSEs are the most important thing in their lives and threatening children with a poor life if they don't do well in their exams.
- Insisting the autistic child has to be treated like everyone else. This contravenes the Equality Act 2010.

> *I zone out of long talks or even long sentences. I can't remember more than two sentences. Teachers say one thing and then do something else. They change things and I get in trouble for losing focus and being distracted.*
>
> *(Autistic child, aged 12)*

> *They would push and push for me to get back into class when it was not possible for me. After teachers were given instructions to sit me at the back of class many ignore this and put me at the front thinking they could help me when they should have listened to me and the pastoral team.*
>
> *(Autistic child, Spectrum Gaming)*

COMMUNICATE WITH YOUR SCHOOL SENCO

Being a secondary Special Educational Needs Co-ordinator (SENCO) is one of the hardest jobs in education in that it is the only role that has statutory obligations on monitoring and supporting SEND children and the requirement to be educated to Master's level in the SENCO qualification. A child with an Education, Health and Care Plan (EHCP) has the legal right to have the support outlined in that document, but it is subject teachers who will need to implement that obligation. The SENCO has to report progress and continuing needs annually; this too is a legal obligation. Now consider that, in many schools, the SENCO is not on the Senior Leadership Team (SLT) (despite it being a national recommendation in the SEND Code of Practice), they are often left in a wilderness between subject teachers and the leadership team. It is the SENCO's job to speak up to the SLT for the resources needed and pass on training and information to the subject teachers that will teach a child with SEND. On top of that, they are responsible for the collection of assessments and the paperwork involved in applying for support, organising the deployment of teaching assistants, and working with parents. As a form, subject or pastoral teacher, please get to know your SENCO well. Find out what wealth of resources and help they can give you and in return, give them the information, assessment data and insights you have about the children with SEND.

USE TEACHING ASSISTANTS WELL

There are many roles a teaching assistant may have in your class. Many secondary schools appoint a teaching assistant that is based in a subject or department so you may get to know those that are connected to the department you teach in. Others are 1:1 with a child (this is less common), and it may not be the same teaching assistant in every lesson. If you have time, I recommend reading the research done by the Education Endowment Foundation on making the best use of TAs (2018). As a subject teacher, these are some practical ways you can make the best use of the usually well-qualified additional adult in your class.

> Use TAs to supplement what teachers do, not replace them.
>
> *(EEF:* Making Best Use of Teaching Assistants, *2015)*

- To work with TAs you need to plan and give some thought to what your whole class is able to do, what they know and how they learn. Discussing this with the TA, you can agree a focus for different children's learning for the topic. For example, agree on what you would like the child to understand and learn and make sure that they will be able to apply this learning by the end of the topic.
- If you are unsure about how best to use your TAs, talk to your SENCO or bring it up as an issue to cover in whole-staff Continuing Professional Development (CPD).
- Be mindful of when the TA may be doing the work for the child just to keep them up with the pace of the lesson. This can be developed by changing the focus away from output (creating a piece of recorded work) onto what the child is learning or understanding.

> If TAs have a direct instructional role it is important they add value to the work of the teacher, not replace them – the expectation should be that the needs of all pupils are addressed, first and foremost, through high-quality classroom teaching. Schools should try and organise staff so that the pupils who struggle most have as much time with the teacher as others.
>
> *(EEF, 2018)*

- Plan how your TAs can develop independence in your autistic children's learning. This can be through providing visual supports that the children can refer to as they do a task, teaching them how to use problem-solving structures and asking key questions rather than telling them what to do or what the answer is.
- Some autistic children do need a 1:1 support. I have known autistic children who have achieved well because of that relationship with a key adult they trust and who has worked to build their skills right through to their exams. Consider changing roles with your TA sometimes and you work with the child for part of the lesson. This will be hugely beneficial for the child and your knowledge of their learning.

- When you do your term or topic plan, share it with the SEND department so the TA can have some thinking time of how they might support the child. They can have great ideas and introduce you to new resources that can help all the class. If you haven't had time to do this or there is a change of plan - explain this to everyone at the beginning of the lesson and go through what the new content will be at the beginning.

> If only teachers would tell us what they were going to teach we would be much more effective and able to help the children access the lesson. Sometimes it is so strange and new to us, we are just trying to keep up and can't be much help to the children.
>
> *(A group of TAs, secondary school)*

- If you have some direct teaching or a specific task that the TA could implement with some of your students, train them properly, have good communication and feedback and plan how the progress might be seen in lessons too. This can be a subject specific intervention, such as teaching a set of geography skills, vocabulary catch up in science, understanding and reinforcing a specific maths topic, or inference skills in English. Knowing what impact this is making is important and can be very valuable to their final results.

7

MORE ABOUT LEARNING

EXECUTIVE FUNCTIONS AND MONOTROPISM IN AUTISTIC CHILDREN

The concept of 'executive function' refers to the higher order control processes necessary to guide behaviour in a constantly changing environment (Jurado and Rosselli, 2007). The concept includes abilities such as planning, working memory, mental flexibility, response initiation, response inhibition, impulse control and monitoring of action.

Executive function skills affect every subject and are challenged by all the moving from class to class and from teacher to teacher each day. They can use up a lot of 'spoons' for the autistic child. They get disciplined and given detentions for not having things or not being able to work out what to do. They struggle with time and are late or early to everything, and their working memory is affected too.

Recent theories have described how monotropic processing is a feature of how many autistic people process the world around them. This means that their attention may be more focussed on specific areas of interest, things they notice and are motivated by. Monotropic processing is used to explain why autistic people often have what seem to us to be narrow and rigid interests and thought patterns. They may seem obsessed by a particular topic, or only able to focus on certain details, rather than seeing the bigger picture (Murray, Lesser and Lawson, 2005). For them it is a strength, an ability to learn something in depth and gain joy from knowing and doing something that they are passionate about. Being monotropic can impact on their language

DOI: 10.4324/9781003280071-10

processing, especially when language is coming from multiple sources or social interactions, and it also impacts on their ability to switch their attention to something else. There are many demands on autistic children to do these things in school. When teachers interrupt a child working on a task, it can disrupt their ability to refocus on the task. Some autistic children have to finish a task before moving on to something else and can become very distressed if we insist that they will be able to finish it later. Neurotypical children can usually work in a polytropic way, being able to give attention to multiple items and ideas at the same time. We tend to teach to this approach and expect that children can make the links, switch attention and work with multiple ideas and topics to generalise their learning.

As we consider autism as a different operating system in the brain, we can see that some autistic children may have some difficulty predicting an expected course of action in an ever-changing classroom. Autistic children often tell me that in order to do something, they need to know what they are doing and what the purpose of it is. The 'why' is really important to them. There are equally autistic children who struggle with huge anxiety because making mistakes or being told off becomes a huge, all-consuming fear, every day at school. There may be autistic children who are very well organised and whose executive functions are well developed that still struggle with switching attention from task to teacher, subject to subject. However, this emphasises the importance of knowing each child's individual strengths and needs. To be honest, I've never known a child's executive functions or attention improve by being told off, nagged or disciplined. Along with fidgeting and stimming, they are fundamental brain differences that need support and teaching. Quietly and routinely provide the support they need, so you can get on with your lesson and they can focus on what you are teaching them. In many autistic children, organisational skills usually need much more scaffolding and support that in neurotypical children. We often support them by cueing them in, specific teaching, visual reminders and walking through the skill with them time and time again until it becomes a routine.

Change can be a huge stress factor for autistic children. These can be small changes, like using equipment in a different way, or they can be larger: a change of room or teacher can cause meltdown in some autistic children. There are many courses of action and possible responses depending on the context, and all the possible variables could be flowing through the autistic child's thoughts, either rendering them unable to respond or rushing to find a familiar and controllable action (such as repetitive stims or actions). Some autistic children have a different concept of time; their anchor points in the day may be quite different to what teachers assume are important to the class, and they can struggle to predict what something will be like as the familiarity with similar activities may not be the same as what you may be thinking. For example, a child may have sensory anchor points, such as 'going past the dining canteen smells a certain way depending on the time of day.' Some things that are OK sometimes may be intolerable at other times and this is not as predictable as you may think. What an autistic child gives attention to may be more specialised and focussed on a narrower version of the bigger picture that you want them to see.

> Attention is the resource which is competed for by task demand, and a task is an enacted interest. In order to perform a task (as a task) any individual needs to:
>
> - see the point of the task - understand the goal
> - value the point of the task - be motivated by it
> - see how to perform that task - understand precisely what task it is, what steps must be taken to carry it out
> - know how to take the identified steps.
>
> *(Murray, Lesser and Lawson, 2005)*

Some children develop these executive function skills more slowly and unevenly than in neurotypical development, and others find that they always will have these challenges. To blame a child for not being able to do something they are not developmentally able to do is wrong. These executive function challenges are very common in pupils with attention deficit hyperactivity disorder (ADHD) too, and many autistic children have a dual diagnosis of autism and ADHD. As teaching staff, if we look out for where a child needs that scaffolding, the independence may only come when they learn to manage that strategy themselves, rather than developing the skill without the support.

Structure and meaning are important to autistic children. Familiarity and predictability are anchor points for them to manage in a largely unpredictable world. Our assumptions about what children should be able to do, or should know what to do, should be questioned. We should try to look at it from the autistic child's point of view. **Do they know what they should do? Do they know why? Do they know how to do what you have asked them to do? Are there any barriers to doing that for them?**

> *My brain just doesn't work in the same way as other kids. I can think about how a black hole is made in minute detail, but can't remember if there is a pen in my bag or what books I need for the day. For years I've been carrying everything in my bag everyday. I still worry and stress constantly in case I have forgotten something.*
>
> *(Autistic child, aged 15)*

Some autistic children do develop more tolerance and choose to take on the challenge of joining in something they previously found difficult, but often that comes as a result of the adaptations and understanding you gave them first. The increase of an autistic child's confidence from the ages of 11 to 16 can be a joy you have been privileged to contribute to.

TEACHING VOCABULARY

Autistic students are all different. I may have said this before! But when we have a range of children in our classes the range of vocabulary they may know or be able to use and understand in our subject will be wide. Autistic children can have interests and enthusiasms that they love to learn about and use that monotropic focus to learn all they can about that subject or character. I know autistic children who have known more facts about a curriculum subject than the teacher and easily get bored by having to go over things they already know. Other autistic children have missed or not yet developed the vocabulary they need for a subject. This can be because they have learned and developed in a different way than the taught curriculum (which is based on neurotypical development) or that they have not been interested, have not had the right explanation or haven't been taught how to understand and use the vocabulary in a way that makes sense to them. Much of the current research on vocabulary teaching is relevant to autistic children, but needs to take into account their different ways of processing and learning language; however, autistic learners are rarely mentioned in this research. If we get to know the way an autistic student learns and works with language, we can use this to our advantage.

- Teach word meanings specifically. Allow students to look word meanings up electronically if that works better than a dictionary. Check your language is concise and direct, not ambiguous and where there is more than one meaning, explore what they are.
- Teach the context of words and remind them how to work out a word meaning from the context. Use visual clues such as highlighters to keep track of words in text.
- Use visuals to back up the learning of new vocabulary. A good visual helps the child remember the meaning of the word alongside learning the word. A mind-map of key subject topic vocabulary with pictures relating to the words can be useful to support a child through a topic. Include a list of 'doing words,' those words that tell us to do something that are generic across all subjects; e.g., 'explain' means ... If there is subject variation in these words, explain why. Give an example, in context to go alongside it.
- Show them vocabulary mistakes in other people's work (not current classes), using examples where the word would be used wrongly and explain why. There are probably a lot of examples in the media to draw from.

- Modify your approach depending on the child's knowledge and strengths. Ask them what they know at the beginning and ask them to explain it to you. Some may know things they cannot explain, and this does put them at an advantage in exams. Practising and scaffolding this will help them.
- Don't overwhelm them with too much vocabulary to process at once. Give them time to learn and embed, practice and apply the vocabulary. Some autistic children can find it difficult to generalise from one subject or topic to another. Don't assume they know something in a new context until you have explained that link.

> *It was maths and I didn't understand what the questions meant and the way it was phrased so I got stressed. They took me to the super easy group which didn't actually help. It was the wrong help because I could do the maths, I just didn't understand the way they asked the questions.*
> *(Autistic child, Spectrum Gaming)*

EXPLAINING CONCEPTS AND LINKS

All subjects have a story that is woven through the curriculum. As teachers, we know the story; we know the invisible links and the bigger picture that pulls all that knowledge together, and over the five or so years we teach that subject to a cohort of children, we seek to help them see that for themselves. Ultimately the final exams test the child's ability to bring all their learning and understanding together, but I know most teachers want the children they teach to understand their subject for life, to use their foreign language skills, to speak confidently in different settings based on the skills they learned in drama, be able to cook and plan a healthy menu for life from what they learn in food technology, and so on.

Autistic children may not naturally pick up the bigger picture and make those contextual links. This can be due to their focussing on details (monotropic attention), or because you haven't explained what the links are. They may be struggling to listen because the lesson is too noisy or the sensory overload is affecting their learning and they miss some vital information. **What is obvious to you may not be obvious to them, and they may not understand that the things they are being taught are meant to connect together**. If you get into the habit of explaining the links and subject concepts to your pupils, consider adding an extra layer of visual mapping for autistic pupils.

Hilary Forbes, an autistic maths teacher, says that a lot of our curriculums (in her case, maths) assume a lot of contextual understanding from students.

> *In teaching, it is easy to move seamlessly from concrete to abstract, but it is also easy to forget that children do not always know where that seam lies. This is a crucial aspect of teaching if autistic learners are to grasp the necessary connections. The best way to ensure more explicit connections is to try to understand every possible angle from which the subject matter can be learned. This can be done by getting into the habit of asking yourself a series of questions.*
>
> *Here are some questions that you could consider when teaching any child, but especially autistic children. Of course, they are particularly pertinent to the types of maths problem-solving we encourage all children to explore throughout their maths education.*
>
> - *What could be misunderstood?*
> - *What words or phrases are there that need explaining?*
> - *Are there everyday words used in the subject matter that mean something different in maths?*
>
> (Forbes, 2022)

MARKING AND FEEDBACK

Autistic children can benefit from specific feedback, which first outlines **what it is they have done well**. This sets up the foundation from which to manage any corrections or editing. We often find that autistic children struggle with accepting feedback and making corrections or improvements to their work. Other autistic children are perfectionists and will work and work, never satisfied or accepting that a piece is finished. You may think this is desirable in your subject, but this difficulty can lead to a lot of anxiety to the point of self-harm and mental ill health. Our autistic children often find homework very difficult because the time teachers have to mark it (and the feedback they give) is minimal.

To make marking and feedback effective, have a conversation with each autistic pupil and ask them what they think. Ask them if they are able to use what you say to improve their work and if what you give makes sense to them. If you find that they are very anxious and cannot accept feedback or corrections, try starting by giving them a piece of your work to correct. It is also better to pick out clear, direct points, such as "add more descriptive words," "the diagram needs more labelling words" or "I want to read about the characters' feelings in your work." I have known a number of autistic children who made much more progress when teachers started to tell them what they had done right. They were also more willing to make the corrections that made the work a better piece.

> *In regards to marking etc. I never got clarifications on what the improvements I should've been making meant. The one time I asked my science teacher why I hadn't received full marks, as in her own words I'd done nothing wrong and everything right, I was told I would have "nothing to aim for" if I got full marks so they wouldn't give me them. Why would I bother at that point when I knew no matter how well I did, I wouldn't be graded properly?*
>
> *(Autistic child, Spectrum Gaming)*

GROUP WORK

Think back to Hilary's account of group interactions in Chapter 2. In any classroom there are often more than seven people to interact with. We may ask children to work in groups and then expect them to know how to get on with it and work together.

For an autistic child, this can be a nightmare. Not only do they have the amount of interactions to attend to and switch their attention to, but there is often intolerable background noise from other groups and many other sensory demands.

In a school I often suggest that the teacher supports the autistic child to work with just one other person. In a pair, they can be much more successful in sharing ideas to get the task completed. You may need to teach or structure the task in a way that each child knows what their role is and what they are expected to do or produce. Learning to listen to each other and deal with differences of opinion or ideas is a challenge in itself (for both children in the pair). Many secondary children I work with say that school life would be much better if teachers would let them work on their own or in a pair on shared tasks, rather than making them work in a group. Please consider what Hilary says about groups and the number of interactions when you are planning shared tasks to do in your lessons. And make sure the person they work with is someone who will work well with them. Some children will get better at working in groups that are calm and well structured; others may take all their effort just to work with one other person right through to the end of their school days (McCann, 2020).

HOMEWORK

I don't know what your approach to homework is; whether you give it out because you have to or whether you believe it truly helps a child learn your subject better.

> There is no conclusive evidence that homework increases student achievement across the board. Some studies show positive effects of homework under certain conditions and for certain students, some show no effects, and some suggest negative effects.
>
> *(Trautwein and Koller, 2003)*

However, in other research (done with neurotypical children) there seems to be evidence that homework that is clearly explained and where students understand the connection to the class learning can have benefits - although the validity of even this evidence is low (EEF, 2021).

Homework is one of the biggest issues we have to deal with when we support secondary autistic students. If you have a student refusing homework, or never seeming to do homework, or parents who are saying that it is causing meltdowns and great distress, or the student is always in detention for homework not being done, or their homework is of poor quality, here are some things to consider.[1]

We don't find it helpful to start with "Not doing homework is not an option" (this often comes from the Senior Leadership Team (SLT)), because that immediately clashes with the requirement to meet the child's needs.

Homework is desirable and necessary as students work towards GCSEs, as we know. So, what should happen is the making of a plan to work up to achieving homework success.

- First, you have to evaluate what the barriers are to homework for the pupil. They could be any or all of the following bullet points, plus additional factors that you may find out, such as family bereavement, poverty and other life experiences.
- Rigid thinking pattern - "school is school/home is home," not having the energy, and not being able to accept that homework is the part of school you do at home.
- Sensory stress - after keeping it together all day, they just have to let go of that stress at home and are in no fit state to do homework.
- Comprehension - does the student really understand what they have to do for homework? Have they copied it down correctly? Has the teacher explained it in a way they can understand?
- Executive functioning skills - has the student got the organisation, planning, self-monitoring, predicting and working memory skills to be able to do homework independently? Auditory processing difficulties are common in autistic pupils, they may only catch odd words in the verbal

instructions and so never be able to write the homework down properly.

- Fear of failure – schools are so quick to impose sanctions on autistic students who don't do homework that it sets them up for constant failure and then there is no desire to try as they fear the sanctions and it becomes a self-fulfilling prophecy. So many of my students start being given detentions as part of the schools' rigid behaviour policy. This is not taking into account their Special Educational Needs and Disabilities (SEND).

Here are some of the strategies we have tried successfully:

- Sit down with the student and the parent and discuss what the barriers might be. Then explain that homework is something important, but you are going to make a stepped plan together to enable it to be successful.
- Remember homework must have a real purpose, not be just a time-filler so that the teacher has fulfilled their objectives, such as showing senior management that they always set homework. Autistic students need to see the point of what they are doing (and other students do too, I would suggest).
- Let all teachers know the plan – that their responsibility is to make sure the pupil understands and can achieve the homework. This may have to be adapted at first. Structured activities or projects based on their interests work best, rather than open-ended activities. Differentiate the sanctions – so if the student can show they have tried, they don't get detentions.
- Help the student learn organisation skills and, along with parents, discuss together how they are going to organise themselves at home. This may require a visual or written timetable, a sand or electronic timer and a reminder that after the agreed time it is OK to finish.
- Speak to parents about creating a workspace that can be set up for a set time each evening and is as distraction-free as possible. Examples include using a cardboard screen to

create a private booth, with a magazine box or a tray to put finished work in.

- Homework clubs are good if the student isn't feeling overwhelmed. Have a clear purpose and build rewards into success; for example, if the homework is done at the club, parents will allow time on computer, etc.
- Sometimes autistic pupils need a reduced timetable and the free periods are used to do homework for the rest of their subjects. This can go a long way to ease stress from too many subjects and homework.
- Social Stories (please use with care and get training if you want to write your own) can be helpful to record what you have agreed. Explain them well and clearly and leave them with the student to remind themselves of the positive support and help they can get. Social Stories are positive and affirming so can help with self-esteem too.
- If writing is a problem, let them do all their work typed on a computer, but insist it has to be printed out or emailed when it is done.
- To make homework successful, start easy, with what they CAN do, and build it up. If there is sensory stress, allow sensory breaks and put these in place throughout the school day. Even very bright students can benefit greatly from these.

Here is a Social Story to explain homework.
This is only to be used to help a child understand about doing homework, not as a contract to make them do it, especially if they are struggling, anxious or cannot do it because it is confusing to them.

I can do my homework
My name is _______ and I am in Y__ at ___________ High School.

Most teachers in high schools give their pupils homework. I usually get different homework each day. The teachers usually ask us to write the homework in our planner so I know what to do and when it has to be given to the teacher.

Homework is given to help us remember what we learn and see if we can find things out. Sometimes we have to work on the computer, sometimes we have to write or draw and sometimes we have to make something.

It is part of being at secondary school that the children in the school get homework.

It is a good idea to try to do my homework when I get home from school. If I am doing something else, I can decide what time I will do my homework and try to keep to it.

It is good that my parents and maybe other people in my family will help me.

It is OK when I don't like having to do homework. Many children feel like that too. I can try to do the best I can and do a good job because my teachers will expect it to be done no matter how I feel about it!

If the homework is confusing, I could ask my parents if they can understand it. I could see my teacher or teaching assistant and ask them to explain it in smaller chunks. If I have tried to do the homework and it is still confusing, I could get my parents to write a note to explain that I did try and that it was too difficult. This is OK. Explaining is better than hiding it and not saying anything.

When I have done my homework, it is a good idea to put it in my bag the night before so that I know I will have it to give to my teacher on the right day! Some children find it helpful to put the homework dates on a calendar or in their phone calendar, with a reminder.

I can plan a nice treat for when I have done my homework. I could plan my play, to relax or ____________________. Then I will enjoy it, knowing that my homework is done!

NB. It is important to add illustrations between the chunks of text. I often ask the children to find clipart or icons online so that they are personalising the story.

I have used and implemented all these strategies and schools have seen students build up to doing more homework, more successfully. However, I will say that **sometimes homework just has to be suspended for the sake of the student managing and coping with the rest of the school day**. This may be for a set time, or for the whole of their school lives, but we have to remember that we are supporting a child with a SEND and that is their need. And to be truthful, we have had students get through their GCSEs never having done any work at home. Thanks to the flexibility of their school and support from teachers, they have been given the adaptations they have needed to get through. It is the disapplication from homework that has made a huge difference to many autistic children I have worked with. Their mental health is at risk, and taking this huge stressor out of the equation means that a child may be able to manage more in lessons during the day.

NOTE

1 Taken from my blog, https://reachoutasc.com/autism-and-homework/.

8

REVISION, TESTS AND EXAMS

Revision is often a confusing concept for autistic children and they may find that the traditional ways of doing revision just don't work for them and the way they learn. The key approach is individual flexibility. If you are a subject teacher, you are rightly focussed on your subject. It would help you if you had an idea about the other subjects the child is taking. This is so that you can establish whether it is the subject that the child is struggling with, or whether it is executive function difficulties, mental health, anxiety or other issues that are affecting all their subjects.

> *My Head of year in my final year and my Drama teacher through GCSEs were extremely helpful, they both gave support where it was needed and had an understanding of how I felt, my Drama teacher provided me with a safe space to go to when I was not doing great and my Head of Year always was available to chat and listen.*
>
> *(Autistic child, Spectrum Gaming)*

Class tests cause a lot of anxiety in autistic children, often to the point of sleepless nights, difficulty getting into school and meltdowns. Some of the difficulty is the perceived importance and the pressure of time to get it all done. Some autistic children find it difficult to move through the questions, shift attention from topic to topic and to know how much to write. The ambiguity of questions such as "can you explain … ?" may mean different things in different subjects. And if they are a literal thinker, the answer could just be "yes." Literal interpretation of questions is common in autistic children and in the times I have supported autistic children in tests, this has been something

DOI: 10.4324/9781003280071-11

I have noticed. Tests are not usually designed in an autism-friendly way and so often do not provide an accurate picture of what they know. Adaptations such as extra time can be helpful for some and sometimes splitting the test into smaller chunks and doing it over a week instead of in one lesson can be much more successful. Give the autistic child the notice they need. Sudden tests, or tests that are announced the day before can be alarming and hugely distressing for autistic children. Check with them what they prefer and talk to them gently about why you are doing a test. Make it part of your normal way of working and this can help many autistic children prepare for their GCSE exams.

Revision is often a difficult area for many children, but we have found that if we explain what revision is and that it is a way for them to train their brains in how to remember what they already know, we have much more engagement in doing revision. I have produced a booklet explaining what revision is and all the different ways there are to revise. Once autistic children understand this and realise they can do revision in a way that suits them, they are often more willing to participate. Supporting the anxiety, helping them organise and exploring exam concessions early enough to help them realise what help will be there for them can all help them achieve what they are capable of in the exams.

One area to think about is not to under-estimate what an autistic child could achieve. Some may achieve excellent exam results. One autistic student told me she loved exams because she finally got to work in a silent room! Other autistic children may not manage the exams at this point in their lives. I have known autistic adults achieve their GCSEs and go on to achieve degrees years later than their peers. We must be careful not to tell our autistic students that not doing well in these exams will affect their whole lives. This is not true. I have dealt with so many problems that are caused by teachers saying things they think will motivate (or scare) children into working hard that are taken literally by autistic children and lead to them having huge anxiety, depression and fears that they don't need to have. They should be encouraged to understand that they can study as an adult, learn new things and go into careers that use their skills and interests. The range of abilities and difficulties will be wide, varied and wonderful. Working out how they can thrive in who they are should be more important.

> *I left school feeling a failure. I just couldn't do exams at that time. Years later I went to college and did my maths and English, passing both with B's. My next ambition is to get to university and work with autistic children.*
>
> *(Autistic adult)*

> *I achieved 8s and 9s in my GCSEs but the cost to my mental health was high. I developed anxiety and an eating disorder because food was the only thing I could control. My teachers thought I was fine.*
>
> *(Autistic child, aged 17)*

Helen was bullied in Year 8 and could not get back into normal lessons after that as the perpetrators were all in those lessons. Her mental health deteriorated and her parents and the school worked hard to find a way through this for her. They had a class set up for children who struggled to go into normal lessons, called The Bridge, and this was staffed by a teacher who liaised with Helen's subject teachers to get her work. Helen is highly intelligent and for Years 9 and 10 basically taught herself. I supported her to get her autism diagnosis in this time, which meant that everyone now understood her difficulties and anxieties better. There were many frustrations along the way and the thought of taking GCSEs almost caused her to stop going to school altogether. With a flexible approach, she was given a reduced timetable, the opportunity to drop subjects and focus on those she felt she could do, and a plan was made for her to take her GCSEs at home. The school applied for registration of her home as an exam centre, arranged a familiar person to invigilate and made accommodations, such as she was allowed to listen to music whilst doing the exams in a specially set up room in her home. Despite a few wobbles, she took most of her exams, but did not manage to do the last three. Helen achieved 6s and 8s in all her subjects due to this support and her own determination and hard work. This is an extreme example, but more common than you may think. The flexibility of the school and the teamwork between Helen, her parents, the school and myself made this happen. I wish she could have had a better experience from the start, but we are often forced to work with an inflexible system. This shows we can change things for one student and how worthy that is.

Exam support ideas before GCSEs:

- Help the autistic child understand how to plan revision with breaks and movement between studying. Make this visual for them to follow.
- Teach exam language and practice questions in smaller chunks so that they have a structure to work through.
- Let the autistic child visit the exam classroom or hall before anyone else and see where they will be sitting. Check there aren't hugely distracting noises like a busy road or a ticking clock. Allow them to wear headphones if this will allow them to focus and filter out background noise.
- Let them know where it fits into their normal routine and when that routine will be back to normal. Use a diary or calendar and show them what will happen the rest of the day there is an exam.
- Extra time can be applied for, but the child may need a lot of practice in how to move on from one question to another. Practice by allowing them to have a visual reminder of how long to spend on each question on their exam desk, or by having an adult give a pre-arranged signal.

- The autistic child may just need someone just to prompt them to move on, or may need access to a reader, a scribe, a quiet room apart from the main exam hall or a sensory/comfort object with them in the exam.
- Explain to any invigilators the arrangements you have made for autistic children so that they don't undo the arrangements you have put in place.

9

BEHAVIOUR AND MENTAL HEALTH

There are many questions secondary teachers ask me about behaviour. A secondary school can have up to 2,000 children and each subject teacher has to follow the rules and discipline policies of the whole school. This, of course, is usually necessary for good order and the running of the school day so that all children can be safe and understand the expected behaviour that keeps them all safe and allows the teachers to teach them. However, policies are written for the neurotypical majority and, as I mentioned earlier, even the UK Government's behaviour recommendations say that accommodations will need to be made for children with Special Educational Needs and Disabilities (SEND), and the laws that frame this are the Equality Act of 2010, the Children and Families Act 2014 and from that, the SEND Code of Practice 2014.

The link between behaviour and mental health is strong. Many autistic children struggle to communicate their needs and can become anxious or distressed to a point where they cannot speak at all. Having difficulty interpreting their emotional state, plus the daily stress of being at school, is often a recipe for poor mental health. **Behaviour is often communication when words can't be found**. In all my years of supporting autistic children, this has been a very useful mantra to help us understand what might be going on when behaviour concerns us.

My work uncovers a lot of mental health needs in autistic children. Teachers who understand them and take the time to form that positive relationship with autistic children in their classes make such a huge difference that you cannot underestimate. It is people more than strategies that make

DOI: 10.4324/9781003280071-12

the difference. Thank you for reading this book and taking the time to understand your autistic children.

SETTING THE SCENE

Autistic children appreciate clear logic. Explaining rules to them, with the reason why that rule is there, may help many autistic children manage to follow the rule as long as it is within their capability to do so. For some, a verbal explanation will help, but others may need a more carefully worded written explanation and for someone to work with them on understanding the effects of people breaking those rules. However, we also need to teach them that sometimes rules are broken and it isn't noticed or acted upon, and at other times a teacher may discipline a whole class when one or two people have broken a rule. It is absolutely OK to question this. Adults do this in political issues, for example. Fairness and clarity are important to autistic young people. It can be challenging for us as adults to make it sound fair, and if we can't, we may have to admit that to a child and explain that.

> *Sometimes you might get told off and it's not fair. I have tried arguing but it doesn't work. Best just to let it pass. But it helps if you have a parent or a TA you can talk to about it. They can help you figure out whether to complain or ignore it.*
>
> *(Autistic child, aged 12)*
>
> *Unless it is serious, then ask to talk to someone and explain it. Your parents might have to explain for you sometimes.*
> *(Autistic child, aged 12)*

WHAT IS FAIR TO ALLOW?

This is something I am asked a lot. What about the other children? If we let one child get away with something, the others will want that too, or they will make a fuss and shout, "it's not fair!"

When we are working with teenagers, it can seem like the whole world is not fair unless it is in their favour. The best thing to do is to address this honestly. Talk to your class about fairness and equity. There are some good diagrams and pictures available to start a discussion. There is an activity where you give a number of children a note with an injury written on it ranging from a cut on the finger to stomach ache and a broken leg. Each comes to you for help and you give all of them a plaster. Then you can talk about whether treating everyone the same actually helps them. Be careful to discuss whether having different needs means that people are 'less' than others, and do equate disability with other protected factors in the Equality Act like sexuality, race and gender. If this is done in form time, PSHE, Citizen lessons or another format, then all teachers in the school should know that this has been done so that they can refer to it. This is about setting a foundation in the whole school, supported consistently by all staff that develops an understanding of how a caring society can work. Spend time thinking about how you will approach fairness and equality in your lessons and have an answer or discussion ready for your pupils. There are some great resources produced by the LEANS project you will find in the Resources section at the back of this book.

As a subject teacher you may just want to know 'what do I allow in my lesson?' And that is where knowing your autistic and other SEND children's needs will be helpful. If a child needs to fiddle or stim to be able to listen, you can allow that and know that they will not disrupt others and will be listening, or you can spend every lesson getting into a conflict with the child as you tell them off or discipline them again and again. A child who needs to move would benefit from you creating opportunities for them to do so. A dyslexic child will benefit from not being asked to read out loud in your lesson. An autistic child who is affected by sensory overload would benefit from having their hood up in class or wearing earbuds to enable them to reduce that overload.

Have high expectations of behaviour but be mindful of the child's disability and what they cannot do. For example, a child with Tourette's may have movements or verbal ticks. An autistic child may not be able to wear a school tie or keep their shoes on all lesson. A child with attention deficit hyperactivity disorder (ADHD) may never be able to sit still for all of the lesson. If there is a problem with other children making fun of them or shouting that they want these things too, that is not the fault of the child who has needs.

HONESTY AND ARGUMENTS

There are some autistic children who seem very blunt and sometimes unkind in the comments they make to others. They may call out, they may point out your mistakes or they may get into arguments with other pupils regularly. We must first see this through an autism lens. For autistic people, truth and honesty are important, and lying is more unusual than in typical children. It will help to have a chat with the autistic child and ask them why something bothers them and what impact it has on them. Then we can explain what impact it may have on others. It works best when we map this out on a piece of paper so they and we can see all the elements of the discussion and make links. It may be that the autistic child is impulsive and struggles to keep their thoughts inside their head. If this is the case, give them a notebook to write them all down. Accept if you make a mistake, and thank them. You can turn it into a teaching point that failure or mistakes are learning opportunities. We may need to set them some boundaries and this can be explained positively and kindly first and foremost. Write it out as an explanation. And do this in the third person so that you are not blaming but teaching the child.

Here is an example of how to write down an explanation in an objective way.

People can keep some comments inside their brains
Sometimes people don't like or get annoyed with what other people do. They might notice that another person makes a mistake or breaks a rule. This is OK. When people feel like that, they might think unkind thoughts.

It is not always a good time for people to say what they are thinking. One time is when the teacher is giving their lesson input. It is a good idea if people can try to stop themselves from saying their thoughts out loud so that they don't interrupt the teacher. They might try to have a think and decide if the thought can be ignored. Maybe the situation has passed, and it isn't important anymore.

If I have a thought or there is something that someone has done that is still bothering me, I can write it down in my notebook and speak to my trusted person at a quieter time. If it is a problem that keeps happening, it is good to report it to someone. They might be able to help.

This is good.

If their comments are rude, racist, sexist or threatening, then someone they trust will need to work through that with them. Often the reason autistic children say these things is because they have heard others say them in school, at home or on the internet, or that they are being bullied and picked on for their differences and are hitting back. Please be aware of the subtle bullying that many autistic children experience. Being called "autistic" is a common taunt and insult in many schools these days. No wonder our autistic children are hurt and angry.

MELTDOWNS AND SHUTDOWNS

An overwhelming response to an intense situation.
(www.autism.org.uk)

A meltdown or a shutdown is the brain's reaction to extreme sensory, communication and social overload. It's not a perfect picture, but one autistic person described it like a computer crash. If you've ever had a computer crash on you, you know that the processor freezes. No matter how many buttons you press, it can't do anything. It cannot take any more input. You have to switch it off and let it reboot.

Meltdowns, where the child is trying to run away, lying on the floor, maybe hitting out, throwing things or screaming, are a reaction to a brain event. The child is in extreme distress and the brain has entered into 'fight or flight' mode. The ultimate purpose is to keep the person safe by fighting or fleeing. But that is not a conscious decision, it is instinct.

But there is also the 'freeze' response. This is where the brain shuts down and the person cannot move or withdraws into a safer place. Often autistic people say that they cannot control, function or even remember what happens when they are in meltdown or shutdown. It is meltdowns we tend to see because they are 'behaviours' and everyone wants to know what to do to stop them; those who have shutdowns are often missed. But, as the survey done by autistic people themselves shows, shutdowns may be much more common.

> *It seems that a huge number of autistic people have shutdowns ...*
>
> *What's a shutdown like? I can explain mine. If you put me under intense social and sensory stress, my brain starts to feel disorientated. I lose the ability to talk. I can sometimes write, though that ability gets very erratic the worse it becomes. I lose the ability to work out how to look after myself, or get myself home in busy streets. There is a sensation of great internal brain-pain/fuzziness. Things can look weirdly big/small when it's happening. Afterwards, I'm totally exhausted and need to recover for a good hour and a half, often longer. It's not in my control, at all.*
>
> (Ann Memmott, autistic adult)

To help a child who may have meltdowns or shutdowns, at school or at home after school, we need to connect the dots between their school stress and the transition to being at home. Blaming teachers or parents, or worse, the child, is common, but really unnecessary. If we work together to provide the understanding and support the child needs, going through the strategies in this book, for example, then we are more likely to prevent many meltdowns or shutdowns. It can happen that a child refuses to leave a class and that you are worried because there will be a new set of pupils arriving soon and your lesson has been severely disrupted. Be calm, reassure them and keep your own anxiety level under control. Make a plan, send the other children out if necessary or call for help to gently guide the distressed child to a safer place.

In case you do need it, here is how I would support a child who is having a meltdown or shutdown.

- Remove all possible sensory stressors. These can be people or objects. Try turning the lights down or seeing if the child will go to a quiet and safe place (preferably you will have shown and prepared a place they will know is safe for them when they are in distress).
- Keep talk to a minimum. Talking is sensory overload and often makes the child even more angry and distressed. If in doubt - just be silent.
- Get whatever help is available. It will need to be someone who understands the child is in distress and not someone who will come and undo all your good work by shouting at the child and insisting they go to the 'exclusion room' as a punishment. This has happened more times than I care to have known.
- Be patient and give them time to recover. Reassure them they are not in trouble, that you will help them get through this and that things can be repaired. But don't talk too much. Some autistic children need the rest of the day to recover, some may feel OK after a shorter time.
- Move on to the repair stage. Reassure them that they are not to blame and that you understand something went wrong, something that was out of their control. Discuss gently what you can do to help them feel better or repair a relationship with another person they may have hurt (this should include the other person acknowledging how the autistic person felt too). As adults, some humility and acknowledgement that we may have contributed can go a long way.

Frequent meltdowns in schools are often interpreted as bad behaviour. With sanctions and punishments piling up, exclusions and anxiety growing on the part of everyone, it can lead to permanent exclusions and autistic children who end up out of school, severely traumatised by the whole school experience. There are a growing number of autistic children who are not able to manage school at all, following placements where they were not understood, and their behaviour labelled as naughty and deliberate. Looking at behaviour through an autism lens illuminates our perceptions of their visible behaviours and enables us to see the communication, sensory, social, emotional and learning difficulties they may be struggling with. These are things we can work to make better for them. If you are a Special Educational Needs Co-ordinator (SENCO), form tutor or pastoral lead for the autistic child, have a plan in place that has key people who can help. People who understand and who the child trusts to keep them safe.

And one last thought ... if the child has not yet received a diagnosis and you think they may be autistic - assess those needs and make those accommodations. You won't harm them and you can monitor what works and what doesn't as part of the Graduated Approach towards a fuller understanding of their needs. The strategies in this book can help children with other needs; for example, those with attachment needs, trauma, anxiety and other neurodiverse conditions.

MANAGING 'SPOONS' OR ENERGY LEVELS

We can help by recognising the limited amount of spoons an autistic child may have. We can help them conserve their spoons to last through the day and we can help them find ways to add to their supply (not as easy as it sounds):

- Give them a chance to leave your class early or don't make a fuss if they are late. Just cue them into where you are up to.
- Look at your environment and see where you can make it calmer and more accessible, considering the person's sensory needs. Blinds on windows, wall displays, lighting levels and seating arrangements can all make it easier to be in your lesson.

- Break tasks and instructions into more manageable chunks, give them visual or written reminders so they can check them and allow them time to do each one.
- Support organisation and set up a communication system where the autistic person can let you know if they are struggling. Be aware that many find this difficult, especially when it demands using a 'communication spoon.' They may not be able recognise that they are struggling until it is too late, but structuring tasks for them, whether through a list, visual schedule, practical equipment or a writing frame, can still help. It will be useful if you can learn to 'read' their autistic non-verbal communication and know when to reduce demands.
- Let the person do activities related to their special interests. If the topic doesn't lend itself to this, then allow them time with their interests once the task is finished. Or just leave them alone for a while to give them time to manage their own regulation; if they miss out on doing one lesson of work, they could still be listening and learning if not put under that pressure.
- Let them request 'time out' or a break. It is important for the autistic person to recognise when things are getting too much for them and they should request a break before frustration and overload lead them to communicate this in behaviours, or reach the point where they cannot cope and meltdown happens. This may not work for some; asking to go out of the lesson means drawing attention to yourself from all the other children and this can be too much for some autistic children. It may be that the 'time out' is a time to sit and doodle at the back of their books for a few minutes whilst they are regulating themselves.
- Let them have alone time at breaktimes if they want to. Or give them alternative things to do, especially at lunch times. Offer your classroom as a sanctuary at breaktimes; let them help you organise your resources or do something they like in your room at times when they need it.

If the person is having a minimal-spoon start to the day, increase the sensory breaks, reduce the social and work demands and expect that they will find it much harder to concentrate.

If you understand the autistic child and they can trust you, they won't take advantage of your adaptations; they will feel safe, understood and be able to cope with more challenges than maybe you thought possible. **Maybe you should keep a couple of spoons on your desk with the person's name on, and remove one when things are not going so well for them**. Then think about how you would cope with just one spoon left and no way of buying any more.

TEACHING RESPONSIBILITY

Another thing I am often asked is how to teach an autistic child to take responsibility for their actions. As they grow up, we may be concerned that they may do something that could get them into trouble with the police and that the 'outside world' will not be as understanding as you may be. It is important to keep the Double Empathy Problem in mind and be aware that autistic people have a right to be understood and not discriminated against. With this in mind, we can teach all children about responsibility.

We can start with a simple map of cause and effect which can help in some situations with some autistic children. Those who like to follow and keep to the rules will often be conscientious to do so when you explain the process and reasons why clearly. Sometimes I use a simple flow chart which can help an autistic child learn something about the effects of their actions. However, it is important that they can use this to communicate the effects of other people's actions on them and see that staff are following the same process to sort it out.

The trouble with this is it is often related to justifying imposing sanctions. It can be more beneficial if we instead teach them about what taking responsibility is, spending the time to work through each scenario and helping the child see the effects of what happens on the people and environment around them. To do this adequately we should start with acknowledging the effects that other people's behaviours are having on the autistic child. This is where visual mapping helps me in doing this work with autistic children.

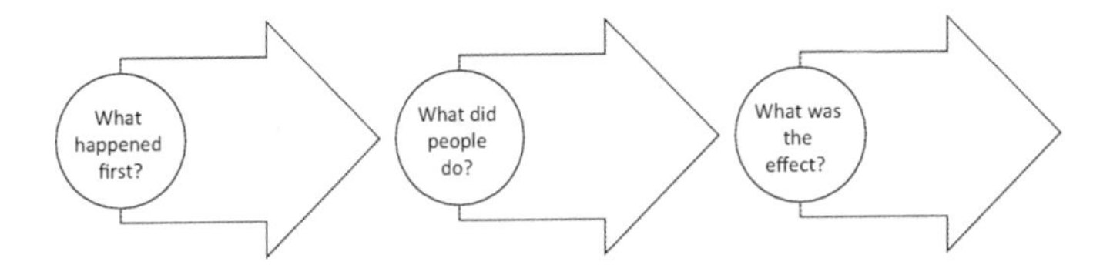

Figure 9.1 Mapping out cause and effect

- First, start by adding to the map what has happened to them. Their opinions and perspectives need to be part of the conversation. The language we use matters a lot.
- Taking out any blaming or accusing language and objectively reporting facts means that we take the pressure off the autistic child.
- Once the autistic child feels listened to, we can move on to looking at what effect the events had on other people. We can explain the social rules we have to keep people safe and the responsibilities of being in a social situation.
- We need to understand the literal perspective of the autistic child, and their need to see things handled logically, from a strong sense of fairness.
- Sometimes it is just that other people are 'getting away with it' and this needs to be understood and discussed.
- Sometimes what seems obvious to us might not have occurred to an autistic child, and at other times they are reacting out of fear and are intensely worried that they will get into trouble without knowing how to control their responses.
- Sometimes autistic children become fearful of what changes you might be asking them to make, especially if it seems like others are not being asked to change. Try to walk through any demands with them, explaining why and how, and giving them clear support and feedback.
- I would recommend watching this sensory overload stimulation to see how reactions that could lead to police involvement could stem from sensory distress rather than not understanding consequences: www.youtube.com/watch?v=K2P4Ed6G3gw.

Of course, autistic people can do wrong things. Their anxiety can lead to abruptness and unkind actions. Some may try to control situations and people without taking into account that other people have needs. Some may not understand something that seems obvious to neurotypical people. But more often autistic people are vulnerable to being taken advantage of by those seeking to exploit them. If we are going to help them understand responsibility, consequences and control, then it will take understanding and a way of communicating this to them that will make sense to them, over a long period of time. In our schools, autistic children, like most teenagers, are growing, learning and maturing through these secondary years and the effort we put in may not show fruit until long after they have left school.

Here are some tips to start this process.

- Work with parents, plan a programme and involve them in what you will be covering. Invite them to contribute and share what they worry about for their children, but also share the way you are approaching this so that they can follow it up with their child at home.
- Use visual mapping to explore situations and events as above. Make sure you start with the perspective of the autistic child. Use this format often and build it up as a usual way of working through problems and scenarios that are important to them.
- Some parents say their child will communicate through text or email, which gives them more time to think and process what to say. Try to develop time to process and explore the best communication methods for each child.
- Explain the key terms and go through it with them until the children have a working definition that you can refer back to and adapt as necessary. Responsibility, different types of consequences, rules, laws and justice are important terms.

Additionally:

- Have an autistic police officer come to talk to your autistic children. There is the autistic police national network: www.npaa.org.uk.

Why is it difficult?

- Too many people talking at once.
- I know what to do and they don't have as good ideas as me.
- I'd rather work on my own.
- I hate writing.
- we end up arguing.
- It makes me really angry.
- It is stressful.
- I want to do a good job.

What do the other children say?

- We have good ideas too and we want to see them happen.
- We don't know when to speak or when to listen when lots of people want to talk at once.
- We want to do a good job too.
- We think she has good ideas and we like her being in our group.
- It upsets us all when we argue.

Why do we do group work?

- It teaches turn taking, waiting and listening.
- It helps us learn to cooperate.
- It teaches us teamwork.
- Shared ideas often makes something better.
- Working on a project together can be like the world of work.

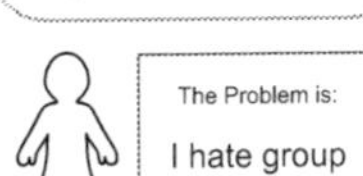

The Problem is:

I hate group work.

My teacher has noticed.

- The background is too noisy with many groups all working at the same time.
- I've not made it clear enough for each person should be doing.
- The children seem unsure how to use different ideas within the group.
- Maybe the tasks are too openended.
- It becomes stressful for a number of children.
- They could organise group work better.

What are the main barriers?

1. The way the groups are organised.
2. Too many people in a group.
3. Trying to concentrate with all the background noise.

How can we make this better?

- Let me know when there is group work happening.
- Let me work with just one other person at a time.
- Let me choose the person I want to work with.
- Give us each a clear job so that each of us know what to do.
- Show us how to share our ideas and workout how to choose the best one.
- Let us work in a quiet space.
- If I am struggling let me work on my own.
- I can tell my friends how to support me.

Figure 9.2 Problem solving map example

- Have autism-specific talks about county lines, modern slavery, sexual exploitation and relationship responsibility. Talk about selling drugs and who is responsible in the law. Do this over time and always start with what the children already know.

Mark was aged 15 when I was working with him and he declared to me that as soon as he would turn 16 he was going to visit a prostitute. He was talking about it around school a lot. He had heard that it was their job, so logically and lawfully he would be able to experience sex by visiting a prostitute. He had heard the other boys talk about losing their virginity and that 'everyone did it.'

Mark first talked to me about his point of view, which included the above and the fact that he was scared because he didn't know if sex would upset his senses. He didn't like being touched, but was also scared that the other boys would bully him if he didn't do it.

We then talked about the 'job' of a prostitute and why people might end up doing this job. We included sexual slavery, poverty and pimps. All put on the map, alongside his reasons for wanting to do this. We then used part of the page to explore what girls might think and feel when they heard boys talking about them being available for sex and this led to Mark showing great empathy and understanding of how demeaning it was to them.

He then declared he was not going to visit a prostitute and we discussed ways he could respond to the other boys when they teased him. I think he went away to educate them!

As you can see, teaching responsibility is not a simple matter but, if provision can be made to train pastoral staff, form teachers and SEND staff in how to do this, we are giving our autistic children a huge gift to keep them safe in their adult lives.

PUBERTY AND IDENTITY

Autistic children go through puberty as most teenagers do. Physically there is no difference unless a child has a medical reason for not going through puberty. However, some research says that autistic children may take longer to develop maturity in emotion and perspective-taking than neurotypical children. In my experience, autistic children are as different in the way they experience puberty as neurotypical children, but there are some common considerations we should take into account as teachers.

RELATIONSHIP AND SEX LESSONS

Relationship and sex education lessons in most secondary schools are not designed with autistic children in mind. I have done a lot of work with autistic children undoing the damage caused by making them attend the sex and relationships lessons that everyone else had to attend. This is because:

- The assumptions that the lessons often have about what children already know cannot be assumed for autistic children.
- Autistic children often have a literal interpretation of what is said and need time to explore and understand the concepts in a way that makes sense to them.
- The neurotypical social norms that form the curriculum can cause many difficulties later for autistic children because they are not their way of socialising and may find it hard to do things in the same way as assumed by neurotypical teachers.

DOI: 10.4324/9781003280071-13

- Autistic young people are vulnerable to sexual abuse and exploitation. I have read many accounts and studies that highlight the vulnerability of girls and boys who are autistic. Many of our Relationships and Sex Education (RSE) curriculums do not address these particular vulnerabilities.
- Working with parents on this topic is crucial. Fortunately, there are some very good resources available now that can help teachers teach RSE lessons that are more direct and useful for autistic young people. The list of books and websites is in the Resources Chapter.
- We can assess the autistic children's knowledge, understanding and capacity to interpret this topic. Ask parents what they are doing to support these topics and use good resources with the whole class, but maybe consider arranging for some smaller groups for children who need a more bespoke approach. I have taught RSE to small groups of autistic children in secondary schools and engaging them in discussions about sensory issues, social vulnerability, safety and privacy has worked really well.
- Consider that some autistic children can be very naive and may not be 'streetwise' in many ways. They may explore or talk about issues or sexual content in the wrong contexts, such as in front of teachers, when all they are doing is repeating what other children know not to say in front of adults.

> Girls who score above a cut-off on a screening test for autism are nearly three times as likely to experience sexual abuse as those who score below it.
>
> *(Ohlsson et al., 2018)*

MISINTERPRETATION, OR LITERAL INTERPRETATION

The way we talk about puberty, sex and relationships can be hugely confusing for autistic children. They are disadvantaged by the assumptions that we make. For example, one autistic child was teased by a teacher suggesting in jest that he was going out with a girl he had been staring at. The girl was embarrassed, but the autistic boy spent weeks being extremely anxious that he seemed to be going out with a girl he barely knew, and that he had missed some vital knowledge that even the teacher seemed to know about him. It took a session with me to unpick what had been said to reassure him that he wasn't in a romantic relationship with the girl and had in fact only been fascinated by the badge on her blazer when he had been staring at her.

> *When they told us that our voices were going to break, I was terrified. My mum eventually told me it just meant that the changes in my voice box would make my voice sound deeper and that it was perfectly normal.*
>
> *(Autistic child, aged 13)*

SENSORY CHANGES

The hyper-sensitivities and low-sensitives experienced by autistic children are going to change during the process of puberty.

- Intense pain and emotional distress in autistic girls can be acute when they are menstruating. Autistic girls can also suffer from fear of blood and toilets because of sensory triggers and the fear of what other girls may do or say to them in the toilets. An autistic girl may need access to a more private toilet, such as the accessible toilet in school.
- Emerging sexual feelings are sensory experiences, and masturbation in public (not realising that it is not socially appropriate) may be more common in autistic children. As a teacher, please take this into consideration and, rather than reprimand, take into account that they may need some extra explanation. A boy who is masturbating in class may need a social story to help them understand when and where is appropriate. They may also need some other sensory activity to distract them from the strong sensory urges they have; even a fiddle toy can help, or a period of exercise at breaktime.
- Other sensory needs can change, by becoming more intense or less intense as they go through puberty.

PERSONAL HYGIENE AND APPEARANCE

Autistic children are all different and some are very meticulous about hygiene, some may have associated Obsessive Compulsive Disorder (OCD) and others may struggle to manage their personal care. Speaking to parents and autistic young people, I have realised that there are so many skills involved in this that it can take autistic children longer than neurotypical children to work out what to do and how to do it.

- Telling them to wash, wear deodorant, change clothing or brush their hair is not going to have an effect unless we understand their sensory needs.
- Brushing hair and teeth could be terribly painful for them. Finding alternative ways of self-care might need to be found by parents and allowed for in school.
- They could struggle to organise the process of having a shower or cannot stand the feel of the water from the shower on their skin. Visual schedules can be really helpful so they can see how to do it step by step.
- They may hate the smell and taste of toothpaste, the stink of soap and shampoo and find newly laundered clothing scratchy and uncomfortable. I have had some great lessons looking at personal hygiene and the sensory alternatives to different self-care products and practices with my autistic children in secondary schools.
- If an autistic child has OCD, then the right support is needed to allow them to feel clean and safe. Further information can be found at: www.autism.org.uk/advice-and-guidance/topics/mental-health/ocd/professionals.

PEER PRESSURE

Some people think that autistic children are not bothered by peer pressure as they are unaware of the social nuances of others. This may be true of some, but it is never a good idea to assume one thing for all autistic people. I know autistic children who are followers of fashion, who care intensely about what other people think of them and some who are people pleasers, desperate to fit in and be accepted. Many autistic children in secondary are acutely aware that they are different.

> *Other kids tell me I'm different. They use autism as an insult. I'm terrified of people touching me, it freaks me out, and that's just another reason other kids make fun of me.*
>
> *(Autistic child, aged 12)*

Once you know about masking and the toll it takes, we can see that autistic children are vulnerable to being taken advantage of by others. Just recently, one of my autistic children on his taster day to his new secondary school was told to set off the fire alarm by another child. He was about to do so, because he believed you do what your friends say. Luckily it is an autism-aware school and a member of staff realised what was happening. But already that child is vulnerable to the word getting around that he will do what you tell him. I often advise that if an autistic child does something that breaks the rules, find out why, and don't forget to ask them if someone told them to do it.

AUTISTIC IDENTITY

Being autistic is nothing to be ashamed of and autistic pride is a wonderful thing. Whilst being autistic does have its challenges, being autistic can mean a variety of strengths, talents and weaknesses are present – just like they are for neurotypical people.

- The ability to focus on their passions and enthusiasms, the ability to notice things, think outside the box and be a loyal and dedicated friend are just some of the positives that we might see in autistic people.
- Being artistic or good at cooking, writing and design are as widespread as being good (or not) at maths. The autistic children and adults I have known over the years are all interesting and capable people.
- The problem is that many autistic teenagers get their diagnosis in the middle of a traumatic time. They may have

been in trouble, at the brink of exclusion, very anxious and depressed. They may have been through years of their parents fighting for help and being rejected time and time again by mental health services.

- Having an autism diagnosis should be a joyful relief - at last there is an explanation as to why they are who they are. But sadly, the world around them speaks such negativity, it can take some time to overcome the sadness and fear being autistic makes them feel. One child asked me if autism meant she was going to die.
- As a subject teacher you can do a lot to help. You can include role models of all different kinds of neurology and disability in your subject. From Alan Turing to Susan Boyle to Chris Packham and Greta Thunberg, there are many autistic and neurodiverse people in all fields of study that can normalise the diversity of human beings. I love exploring autistic comedians and dispelling the myths, openly and honestly about what we know about being autistic. You may not have time to spend on exploring this with a child 1:1 as I can in my role, but you can promote positive attitudes to diversity in all its forms.

> *As a pre-teen, I remember being obsessed with the concept of 'normal'. I distinctly remember comparing myself to my classmates and being sure that I was the odd one out. Over time I grew to realise that 'normal' is a harmful myth, and that all the things that made me 'stand out' were the things that made me who I am. I grew to celebrate being autistic.*
>
> *(Dean Beadle, autistic adult)*

GENDER AND SEXUALITY

Currently over 30% of the autistic population identify as LGBTQ+. In our work in the past few years, we have listened to many autistic young people who are exploring and discovering their identity and because we have better vocabulary and an emerging acceptance in our society, our autistic young people are voicing their preferences. It is a joy to just listen, and it is no big deal to use their preferred name or pronouns. Teachers can learn the basics of the language and stories people are telling about their identity so that they are better informed. No matter what your own views are, autistic young people, like all others, are exploring who they are and where they fit in this world. And please don't jump to any conclusions. Often, when we have spoken to those who want to be identified by a different-from-birth gender, they have thought things through deeply, and are rejecting much of society's pressures to act and be a certain way because of their birth gender. Those who are gay or asexual (again, a common identity in the autistic community) need our understanding and acceptance. As a subject teacher, accepting the child, having a positive and friendly relationship with them, makes more of a difference than anything else. I have added some good resources in the resources chapter of this book.

> Leila, aged 16, was excited. She had told her teaching assistant she was gay and had her first girlfriend. The TA chatted to her about it, asking gentle questions to help Leila think about if the relationship was kind and safe. Then Leila wanted to know whether to tell the rest of her classmates, she wanted them to share in her joy and couldn't understand that some of them might make fun of her. With a social story approach, the TA worked through who might be safe people to tell, who were the people she trusted, and suggested that Leila start with these.

RISK-TAKING AND PROBLEM-SOLVING

We know that all teenagers' brains are changing and risk-taking is a skill that is developing, much to our consternation at times!

- Autistic children may be over-cautious and the need to control situations is often linked to their intolerance of uncertainty.
- They can find it difficult to imagine what you are going to do, or what something will be like if you haven't given them enough information. It may be that you have said one thing and now you are doing something else. The anxiety this causes cannot be underestimated.

- Autistic children can be highly creative and willing to try new things if given the right support. This can be as simple as mapping out exactly what will happen and what is expected. It can be developing a tolerance of some uncertainty through carefully examining the possibilities and reassuring autistic children that they are safe to do so.
- It will be helpful to understand that when an autistic child has a diagnosis of attention deficit hyperactivity disorder (ADHD) as well, they can be impulsive and reactive as that is driven by the ADHD. The internal conflict between the two conditions can be the need for control alongside the impulsiveness, which we often see in behaviours that may be sudden and disruptive.
- I teach problem-solving skills to autistic young people by using a visual mapping approach. I follow this kind of structure and all of it is written down so we can look at it again:
    - What is the problem? Write it down so we know what it is we are dealing with.
    - Why is it a problem to you ... and why might it be a problem to someone else?
    - What are the barriers you see are preventing you dealing with or solving the problem?
    - What do you know already?
    - What do you want to happen if it could be sorted out?

After that, we can look at all the factors we have on our piece of paper, and work out a solution from something positive they have contributed. We start with easy to solve problems, such as "someone has sat in your place." Then we can work through problems they have solved before. Eventually we can find an approach to difficult problems and even unsolvable-by-us problems (such as the education system!). Done in a group, this can build debating skills and the willingness to ask others for help.

In one of my sessions, one of the autistic boys, Harry, came into the room very distressed. He shared that there was a boy who was bullying him, and he had just threatened him on the way to the lesson. With the help of the group, we mapped it out and teased out the details. After ten months of teaching the group problem-solving, they got to work and helped Harry work out a plan of action. They identified a key teacher he trusted to talk to, and agreed to look out for him at key times around school so he knew he had friends nearby. The next session he reported that the situation had been sorted out and the boy was no longer bullying him.

BULLYING AND ONLINE ACTIVITY

Bullying is a serious concern for autistic children. I have already talked about how they are picked on because they are different and how they are vulnerable to being exploited by others.

A study reported 62% of autistic children had experienced bullying, such as being deliberately provoked into meltdown, sensory bullying, social exclusion, their social naivety being taken advantage of and cyber-bullying, including fake accounts, public shaming and Photoshopping (IAN, 2014). Sadly, my team of autism-specialist teachers and I listen to stories of these happening to many of our autistic pupils. In my work with helping the anti-bullying charity Kidscape make their resources autism-friendly, we have heard so many stories of autistic children being bullied because they are different and seen as an easy target. Other children have more social competence to make excuses or explain away their actions, and autistic children and their parents often report that schools did not believe them, even blaming the autistic child for bringing it upon themselves. I wish I did not have to write that. I wish I did not have to listen to the ways that autistic children are picked on, left out, persecuted and hurt because they are different. It is often the autistic children who are called 'weird,' imitated when they stim and even tormented by children who know that a certain noise or action is hated by the autistic child. Autistic children are also more vulnerable to toxic friendships, being abused by someone they think is their friend and exploited for their naivety. It is far rarer for an autistic child to be the bully, but in those cases there are often anxieties and trauma at the root of their behaviour which we can work through.

> Forming relationships and understanding what friendship is can be an area of challenge for people with special needs. Social situations can be confusing and parents and educators are often required to help navigate through the minefield that is personal space, eye contact and appropriate conversation. Having a disability can also be a lonely experience, therefore the need to find companionship can be more pronounced, making the person particularly vulnerable to unscrupulous ploys to engage with them and secure their trust. This places an obligation on educators and parents to raise awareness of the existence of 'mate crime' and limit the risk of loved ones being drawn into relationships that may become abusive. What starts off looking like friendship can increasingly become one-sided, and can escalate into physical and verbal assault, intimidation, theft, and even coercion into committing crime.
>
> (Sarginson, 2017)

> *First, we need to understand that autistic children are generally very honest, and very accurate. Few invent stories to get another child into difficulty, and few invent things that have not happened. So, our first step is to presume competence and say that we will take what they say seriously and investigate it properly.*
>
> *(Ann Memmott, autistic adult)*

> *The main challenges I had at school were bullying and the attempt of trying to fit in and failing horribly. Not being able to have the confidence to be myself. Being called "special kid and autismo" on a daily basis. Every day waking up and not wanting to go to school. The little amount of help that actually works. Very little amount of people I can speak to.*
>
> *(Autisitic child, Spectrum Gaming)*

To help an autistic child and their parents when they report bullying:

- Use a visual communication system. There are resources and advice on www.kidscape.org.uk/advice/advice-for-parents-and-carers/what-is-bullying/autistic-children-and-bullying/, which has symbol-based communication mats and strategies to help based on schools and parents working together to make the bullying stop.
- Ask parents to keep a diary of the child's reports of what is happening. Ask them to report facts and how their child interpreted the situation. Reassure them you believe them and set a time to meet for after you have done more investigation.
- Talk to the other children involved. Ask them how they deal with conflict and what problems they have with each other. Often the bullying is other children picking up on the differences and making fun of the autistic child.
- There can be misunderstandings and misinterpretations by the autistic child and the other children involved. Sometimes drawing the story out in a comic strip, using speech and thought bubbles can clarify what happened and what was misinterpreted.
- Bring all the information together and try to share the whole picture with parents without blame. Where reactions and words are malicious, deal with them and teach children what is acceptable and what is not. This does not have to be teaching them that their classmate is autistic, but can be generally about neurodiversity and difference. Where misinterpretation has happened, deal with that through visual comic strips or clear explanations for the autistic child and the other children.
- Try to repair relationships. If the autistic child cannot cope with the other children because of the hurt and anxiety they have caused, then give them time and support them in making new relationships through common interests, shared activities and successful projects. For example, one child built confidence and new friendships by joining the eco-committee at school.

TRANSITIONS

I have done a lot of writing about supporting the transition to secondary school for autistic children and I have seen secondary schools get better and better at this over the last ten years. It starts with the communication between the primary school, parents and the secondary school and building a support programme to enable the autistic child to do any extra visits, meet teachers and prepare for this major transition.

As a form tutor or subject teacher, you may be connecting with the parents of children who have Special Educational Needs and Disabilities (SEND) first on the open evenings as they come to visit your school for the first time. This is a good opportunity to listen; explain that you have some understanding of autism but you know that each autistic child is different. Listening to their concerns, reassuring them that the school is adaptable and giving examples of adjustments that you have made for other children is something that will help parents enormously.

Secondary Special Educational Needs Co-ordinators (SENCOs) will share information about all the SEND children in all the classes you will be teaching and keeping track of their needs and approaches may easily be overwhelming. It is worth using some approaches for the whole class, such as sharing the teaching plan for the subject, sharing visual reminders of expectations and giving yourself time to observe how they work. Getting used to you as a new teacher, even in later years, can take longer for autistic children and so it is worth just taking those extra few minutes to chat with them, find out something they like and check in with them now and again.

Daily transitions can be more stressful than the big changes of moving schools.

DOI: 10.4324/9781003280071-14

It is the day-to-day transitions that get to me the most. I could plan for going to a new school and all that but I couldn't plan for how many times I'd have to change rooms and cope with a new teacher every lesson ... every day. They don't realise how terrifying it is to try and get down those corridors not knowing who else is coming your way or what people might do or say to you. And then if there is a substitute teacher ... well, that's me done in for the whole day.

(Autistic child, aged 14)

In secondary school, my biology teacher helped me get back into my classes when I couldn't attend and would cater to my needs without question, he also wouldn't blame me for needing these changes. He is the only teacher that made me want to learn again.

(Autistic child, Spectrum Gaming)

I asked some of my Year 7 (11–12 years old) autistic children at Ripley St Thomas Academy in Lancaster what advice they would give to new pupils coming to their school the next year. These are just some of their top tips:

Find all the quiet places in school. Places where you can go at break times and you can meet your friends there.

I would try to get out of class quickly and get through the corridors before they get too busy.

I would say, walk with the teaching assistant who helps you or another pupil. Other kids get out of their way and behave when there is an adult in the corridor.

MAKING FRIENDS

I found it best to talk to a person I sit next to. I asked them if they wanted to be my friend on the second day. Then they introduced me to other people so I didn't have to approach them.

Just ask someone what they like, and hope it is something you like too.

At this school there is Mrs B who will help you if you haven't made friends at first. She gets people together and supports them.

I wish we had the lunchtime clubs on this year. I was looking forward to the history club. It's a good idea to join a club where other people have the same interest.

POST-16 TRANSITION

I often find that the students themselves realise in Year 10 (14-15 years old) that they will soon be leaving school. For some, they may be so relieved that it's all they want to think about. For others, it's such a massive change in their lives - after all, being at school is all they've ever known - that the anxiety it causes can seriously impact on their concentration, mental wellbeing and motivation in school. Some are so anxious they cannot bear to talk about it.

The Year 10 and Year 11 autistic children I work with are often very worried about leaving school. However, working with them to explain what leaving will be like, what options they have and developing some plans that enable them to see the way ahead can be really important. If they have an Education, Health and Care Plan (EHCP) then transition meetings should start in Year 9. By the time they get to Year 11, the meetings should be with the college or other establishment they are going to go to; make a plan of support that the student and their parents can contribute to. If they do not have an EHCP their needs are still important, and preparing them for college or apprenticeships is just as important.

As teachers we are probably not the best careers advisors. Many of us have only ever been to school! But, in any subject, it would be a great idea to explore the kinds of jobs, college courses and careers that can link to your subject and, if possible, show how your subject can help them in their everyday lives. Simple connections can support the motivation to keep up with your subject, even when it is something they may have no interest in studying further. Connecting topics to real life situations can also help with retention. A simple example is working out a discount in a sale on a car or how to calculate an energy bill. It is also OK to explore everyday jobs such as being a waiter, shop assistant, refuse collector, plumber, electrician and so on. Talk about how important these jobs are for the communities we live in. Don't downgrade these jobs and talk about how earning money in any job can give us the freedom to choose to live, have hobbies and visit places we've always wanted to. One of the biggest stresses for our autistic children is imagining what life can be like after school. If we talk about adult life normally, the options that are available and how it is OK to choose what they want to do rather than having to fit into another person's idea of what 'successful' means, this will give them confidence. I love having these discussions with my autistic children. We discover their hopes and dreams, ambitions and lovely ideas about things they'd love to do in their lives, and we talk about ways they can make that happen. It also helps them realise that GCSEs are helpful, but not the only way to achieve in their lives.

When doing transition planning we always include their parents' ideas and try to work with a familiar member of staff who knows the student well. With the student, work out a number of choices they have made for the their future. Talk about their aspirations, their favourite interests and subjects they might do well in. I use a decision-making visual to look at the pros and cons of each option, including what grades might be needed (and what option is available with lower grades if relevant). This information is shared with parents, and the family is given time to explore and discuss with their child. I have done this in Year 9 to help a student choose their options, but mainly with Year 10s and Year 11s, depending on the individual.

Use the internet to research the possible colleges and courses the student might be interested in. There are often a few places to choose from, depending on your area. School 6th Forms might be good for some students for familiarity, but for others might be limited on choice of subjects. Every student will need treating individually to find what will work for them.

Find out what apprenticeships are offered and if support is available for their SEND needs. Present that information to the student and their family, and encourage parents to arrange some visits to these places as early as possible. One student I have worked with has been set up with a farming apprenticeship in conjunction with the family, a local college and a local farm. All bespoke for him.

Talk to the student about growing up and teach them some practical life skills, again working together with parents. Using public transport, making phone calls, sending emails, using money and paying for things are really important skills to help them move on from school into post-16 life.

Plan, talk, prepare, visit, familiarise, support and talk positively about the next stage. But don't overdo it. They still have to finish their time at school and some pupils with SEND/autism might not be able to cope with thinking about exams and college. In that case, plan some transition support after GCSEs have finished. One school I worked with brought the student back into school after GCSEs and he worked with his previous teaching assistant (TA) on getting ready for college with great success.

One thing I try to help our autistic children learn that after they finish school life has more choices. We teach them to map out the choices and options they have and leave space for things they haven't considered. We may never see those young people again in our lives, but all of us remember a teacher or two who understood us, helped us through difficult times or inspired us to love a subject. Autistic children are no different in who they remember, but they may also remember the teachers who didn't understand them, and who contributed to the trauma of being misunderstood in school. I hope this book will help you be one of those who they remember with gratitude for all the little ways you were on their side.

12

ADDITIONAL RESOURCES

I understand that, as teachers, we need to understand the children we teach, but we also need resources. When someone has created a good resource that we can use for our pupils, it can save us time and help them learn in the way that works best for them. There are thousands of resources out there and some of them will be just right for your autistic children, and many will not be. I hope that after reading this book you will be able to better pick out what will be an affirming and positive resource for your autistic child, and what to leave well alone!

I have a website, am on Twitter and have a Facebook page where I post trusted resources that I find from my networks and internet searches, and some that we make ourselves. If you'd like to join me, here are the links:

https://reachoutasc.com
https://twitter.com/ReachoutASC
www.facebook.com/ReachoutASC

SOME GOOD AUTISM WEBSITES

https://autisticnotweird.com
www.differentjoy.com
www.pdasociety.org.uk
www.scottishautism.org

AUTISM RESOURCES, BOOK LISTS, VISUALS, TEACHING PACKS

https://autisticgirlsnetwork.org/resources/
https://chatterpack.net
www.ed.ac.uk/salvesen-research/leans

DOI: 10.4324/9781003280071-15

www.autismeducationtrust.org.uk/resources

https://best-practice.middletownautism.com

www.griffinot.com/asd-and-sensory-processing-disorder/

https://reachoutasc.com/resources/

https://occupationaltherapy.com.au/the-top-10-books-on-sensory-processing/

https://padlet.com/spectrumgaming/AutismResources

OTHER LINKS

www.kidscape.org.uk/advice/advice-for-parents-and-carers/what-is-bullying/autistic-children-and-bullying/

www.autisticslt.com/nd-affirmingslt

https://monotropism.org

www.spectrumgaming.net

www.teachustoo.org.uk

AUTISM AND CURRICULUM

This is an old document but really helpful as it goes through each subject to give advice: https://bso.bradford.gov.uk/userfiles/file/Strategies%20for%20accessing%20curriculum%20Full%20document.pdf

REVISION AND EXAMS

This is the Social Story-based booklet about revision that I have written and provided for download: https://reachoutasc.com/wp-content/uploads/2020/12/Revision-booklet-SS.pdf

https://reachoutasc.com/5-ways-to-support-autistic-students-through-exams/

TRANSITION RESOURCES

Advice and resources for SENCOs, teachers, leading transition on my blog: https://reachoutasc.com/what-makes-transition-work-for-asc-pupils/

And a booklet that can be filled in about the school the child is moving to: https://reachoutasc.com/wp-content/uploads

/2020/08/ReachoutASCtransitiontoSecondaryschoolbooklet.pdf

SOCIAL SUPPORT

Social Detectives Pack: https://reachoutasc.com/resources/social-skills-pack/

www.routledge.com/Talkabout/book-series/SMT

The Double Empathy Theory explained: www.youtube.com/watch?v=qpXwYD9bGyU

PUBERTY, RSE BOOKS AND WEBSITES

Blog by Dean Beadle (2022) https://reachoutasc.com/being-an-autistic-teen-navigating-sexuality-by-dean-beadle/

Davida Hartman: www.autismsexeducation.com/about

Books by Davida Hartman: *The Growing Up Guide For Boys; The Growing Up Guide For Girls; Sexuality and Relationships Education For Children and Adolescents with ASD*

Books by Kate E Reynolds: *What's Happening to Ellie* and *What's Happening to Tom*

Books by Mary Wrobel: *Taking Care of Myself – A Health, Hygiene and Puberty Curriculum for ASD*

Online leaflets and videos (easy read picture supported): www.lanarkshiresexualhealth.org/resources/?category=31

Robyn Steward's excellent books on periods and staying safe: www.robynsteward.com/books-and-media

Internet safety is a priority for all pupils but pupils with ASC can be very vulnerable. These are great resources developed for children with ASC: www.childnet.com/resources and www.childnet.com/resources/star-toolkit

MENCAP resources and advice: www.mencap.org.uk/about-us/what-we-think/relationships-and-sex-what-we-think

Alex Kelly and Brian Sains (2009): *Talkabout for Teenagers: Developing Social and Emotional Communication Skills*

Tony Attwood, Isabelle Hénault and Nick Dubin (2014): *The Autism Spectrum, Sexuality and the Law – What Every Parent and Professional Needs to Know*

Shana Nichols (2009) *Girls Growing Up on the Autism Spectrum - What Parents and Professionals Should Know About the Pre-Teen and Teenage Years.*

Free download: www.rsehub.org.uk/resources/puberty-sexuality-for-children-young-people-with-a-disability/

BEHAVIOUR SUPPORT

Paul Dix (2017) When the Adults Change, Everything Changes

BIBLIOGRAPHY

Autistic Not Weird https://autisticnotweird.com/sats/

Beadle, D (2022) https://reachoutasc.com/being-an-autistic-teen-navigating-sexuality-by-dean-beadle/

Beardon, L (2019) *Autism and Asperger Syndrome in Childhood For Parents and Carers of the Newly Diagnosed – Overcoming Common Problems*. Pub: Sheldon Press.

Bobb, V in Bond, C and Hebron, J (Eds) (2019) *Educating Girls on the Autistic Spectrum*. Pub: JKP.

Castellon, S (2020) *The Spectrum Girl's Survival Guide: How to Grow Up Awesome and Autistic*. Pub: JKP.

Centres for Disease Control and Prevention (2021) https://www.cdc.gov/vaccinesafety/concerns/autism.html

Conn, C (2015) 'Sensory highs', 'vivid rememberings' and 'interactive stimming': Children's play cultures and experiences of friendship in autistic autobiographies. *Disability & Society*, 30:8, 1192–1206, DOI: 10.1080/09687599.2015.1081094 https://www.thelittleblackduck.com.au/uncategorized/autistic-play-styles/

Cullen, RL (2018) The autistic language hypothesis. https://www.researchgate.net/publication/327831058_Do_people_on_the_Autism_spectrum_have_an_over_reliance_on_verbal_communication_as_opposed_to_nonverbal_communication_body_language_and_facial_expressions_in_conversation

Department for Education (2022) Behaviour in schools advice for headteachers and school staff https://assets.publishing.service.gov.uk/government/uploads/system/uploads/attachment_data/file/1101597/Behaviour_in_schools_guidance_sept_22.pdf

Diagnostic and Statistical Manual of Mental Disorders, Fifth Edition (DSM-5) (2013) by American Psychiatric Association. Pub: American Psychiatric Publishing.

Education Endowment Foundation (2018) Making the best use of teaching assistants https://educationendowmentfoundation.org.uk/education-evidence/guidance-reports/teaching-assistants

Forbes, H (2022) How autism may affect students' understanding of maths and what teachers can do to help https://thirdspacelearning.com/blog/autism-maths/

Gotby, VO, et al. (2018) *Journal of Child Psychology and Psychiatry*. Epub ahead of print. PubMed https://www.spectrumnews.org/news/girls-autism-high-risk-sexual-abuse-large-study-says/

Gradin, T (2006) http://www.grandin.com/inc/visual.thinking.html

Gray, C (1994) *Comic Strip Conversations: Illustrated Interactions that Teach Conversation Skills to Students with Autism and Related Disorders*. Pub: Future Horizons.

Green, SA, Hernandez, L, Lawrence, KE, Liu, J, Tsang, T, Yeargin, J, Cummings, K, Laugeson, E, Dapretto, M, & Bookheimer, SY. (2019) Distinct patterns of neural habituation and generalization in children and adolescents with autism with low and high sensory overresponsivity. *Am J Psychiatry*, 176(12), 1010–1020. DOI: 10.1176/appi.ajp.2019.18121333

Hanley, AJ, Khairat, M, Taylor, K, Wilson, R, Cole-Fletcher, R, & Riby, D (2017) Classroom displays – attraction or distraction? Evidence of impact on attention and learning from children with and without autism. *Developmental Psychology*, 53. DOI: 10.1037/dev0000271

Higashida, N (2014) *The Reason I Jump: One Boy's Voice from the Silence of Autism*. Pub: Sceptre.

https://assets.publishing.service.gov.uk/media/5c6eb77340f0b647b214c599/374_Implementing_Inclusive_Education.pdf University of Birmingham.

https://educationendowmentfoundation.org.uk/education-evidence/teaching-learning-toolkit/homework

https://livingautism.com/24-quotes-autistic-individuals/

https://www.autism.org.uk/what-we-do/help-and-support/how-to-talk-about-autism

https://www.cdc.gov/ncbddd/autism/hcp-dsm.html

https://www.nurseryworld.co.uk/features/article/eyfs-best-practice-all-about-autism

https://www.tandfonline.com/doi/pdf/10.1080/09687599.2017.1328157

International Autism Network (2014) https://iancommunity.org/cs/ian_research_reports/ian_research_report_bullying

Mason, W (2014) *The Autism Discussion Page an Anxiety, Behaviour, School, and Parenting Strategies*. Pub: JKP.

McCann, L (2019) *Stories that Explain*. Pub: LDA.

McCann, L (2020) https://reachoutasc.com/group-interactions/

McCann, L and Kidscape (2022) https://www.kidscape.org.uk/advice/advice-for-parents-and-carers/what-is-bullying/autistic-children-and-bullying/

Mehrabian, A (1967) cited in: https://www.bl.uk/people/albert-mehrabian

Memmott, A (2016) http://annsautism.blogspot.com/2016/03/shutdown-autisms-hidden-majority.html

Memmott, A (2018) http://annsautism.blogspot.com/2018/12/

Milton, D (2018) https://www.autism.org.uk/advice-and-guidance/professional-practice/double-empathy

Mummytosix blog (June 2018) https://www.theplightofthesendparent.co.uk/teaching-assistants-and-children-with-special-educational-needs

Murray, D, Lesser, M & Lawson, W (2005) Attention, monotropism and the diagnostic criteria for autism. *Autism: The International Journal of Research and Practice*, 9, 139-56. DOI: 10.1177/1362361305051398

National Autistic Society https://www.autism.org.uk/advice-and-guidance/what-is-autism/varying-support-needs

NICE Guidelines (2017) Autism spectrum disorder in under 19s: Recognition, referral and diagnosis https://www.nice.org.uk/guidance/cg128

Robinson, S, Goddard, L, Dritschel, B, Wisley, M, & Howlin, P (2009) Executive functions in children with autism spectrum disorders https://d1wqtxts1xzle7.cloudfront.net/46895006/Executive_functions_in_children_with_Aut20160629-8399

Rose, K (2021) https://theautisticadvocate.com/2018/07/masking-i-am-not-ok/

Sainsbury, C (2009) *Martian in the Playground: Understanding The Schoolchild With Asperger's Syndrome*. Pub: Lucky Duck Books.

Sarginson, K (2017) https://www.parentingspecialneeds.org/article/mate-crime-signs-fake-friendship/

Schuelka, MJ (2018) *Implementing Inclusive Education.* K4D Helpdesk Report. Pub: Institute of Development Studies.

Smitten, R (2021) *The Secret Life of Rose: Inside an Autistic Head.* Pub: Amazon.

Spectrum News https://www.spectrumnews.org/news/social-communication-autism-explained/

Taylor LE, Swerdfeger AL, & Eslick GD (2014) Vaccines are not associated with autism: An evidence-based meta-analysis of case-control and cohort studies external iconexternal icon. *Vaccine*, 32(29), 3623–3629.

Trautwein, U & Koller, O (2003) The relationship between homework and achievement – Still much of a mystery. *Educational Psychology Review*, 15, 115–145 https://www.readingrockets.org/article/key-lessons-what-research-says-about-value-homework

Verhulst, I, MacLennan, K, Haffey, A, & Tavassoli, T (2022) The perceived casual relations between sensory reactivity differences and anxiety symptoms in autistic adults. *Autism in Adulthood*, 4(3), 183–192.

Vermeulen, P (2012) *Autism as Context Blindness*. Pub: AAPC Publishing.

Watson, A (2022, July 22) https://www.learningandthebrain.com/blog/do-classroom-decorations-distract-students-a-story-in-4-parts-2/

Whelton, E (n.d.) https://ausometraining.com/aba-alternatives-social-skills/

Williams, D (1996) *Autism: An Inside-Out Approach: An Innovative Look at the 'Mechanics' of 'Autism' and Its Developmental 'Cousins'.* Pub: JKP.

Woods, R (2017) Exploring how the social model of disability can be re-invigorated for autism in response to Jonathan Levitt. *Disability & Society*, 32(7), 1090–1095, DOI: 10.1080/09687599.2017.1328157

INDEX

Printed in the United States
by Baker & Taylor Publisher Services